motivation

ISSUES AND INNOVATIONS IN EDUCATION

Consulting Editor
JOSEPH C. BENTLEY
The University of Utah

motivation

Ivan L. Russell
Southern Illinois University
Edwardsville

WM. C. BROWN COMPANY PUBLISHERS
Dubuque, Iowa

Copyright © 1971 by
Wm. C. Brown Company Publishers

Library of Congress Catalog Card Number: 70-140114

ISBN 0–697–06080–2

Second Printing, 1971

Printed in the United States of America

Contents

Preface

Over the years, there has been a vast amount of writing and research dealing with the topic of motivation. Thus far, however, much of it either has failed to reach teachers in a form which could be applied, or it has left them thoroughly confused. At a time when many children need the understanding and guidance of their teachers, it is particularly important that every worthwhile finding pertaining to motivation be translated into meaningful terms. A fundamental belief that "motivation to achieve in school is a mode of behavior learned (acquired) out of life's experiences" has influenced the author to provide very real and practical suggestions and applications which teachers will find useful in their daily interactions with students.

Throughout this book, the underlying assumption is that teachers have a two-fold function to perform in relation to student motivation. They must know and understand the motives which activate and direct student behavior so that they can draw valid inferences from what they observe. Next, but none the less important, teachers must strive to increase the impact of the learning experience so as to stimulate and sustain student effort. The first chapter expresses these thoughts more fully, and the next three chapters present an overview of research concerning motivation. The fifth chapter applies concepts in motivation to the school experience and examines several innovations in education for their effect upon the learning behavior of students. This is followed by a discussion of teacher behavior as it can be influential in creating an atmosphere that stimulates students and helps to carry them through the learning episode.

It is the intent of the author to hold one idea above all others, that *carefully selected and conducted experiences can take an unmotivated student successfully through a learning segment and cause him to become increasingly motivated for future learning.* Traditional schools and teaching methods may have to give way to individualized and

stimulating ways of teaching if this ideal is to be accomplished. However, we have within our reach the potential to accomplish the task of
motivating students, and the problems of society and of the school
demand that we take whatever steps are necessary to gain this objective.

Special effort has gone into making this book understandable for
upper-division undergraduates in teacher education as well as for students in graduate and in-service programs. It should be particularly
helpful in the student teaching phase and in methods courses built
around a comprehensive view of the instructional process. In this book,
students of educational psychology will find a more thorough treatment
of motivation than is contained in the usual educational psychology
textbook.

To my wife, Talulah, and my children, Becky and Jesse, I express
my gratitude for their tolerance and help in making this book possible.
To Mary Howard go my thanks for her typing and editing assistance.
Thanks are due to Robert W. Yates for his help in graphic design.

I. L. R.

1

Motivation:
An Educational Problem

In our vague, rose-colored memories of the yesterday of teaching, the role of the teacher was a simple one—"to teach." The child's role, as it is likewise remembered, was to sit quietly, disturb no one, do the assignment, and absorb the knowledge flowing from the teacher and from one or two well-worn textbooks. Were things ever as simple and easy as that? There were failures—millions of them—boys and girls who elected to cut out long before they reached age sixteen. In the home, school, and community, it was an adult world—children were ignored. And if they demanded attention, they were put down until they either gave up or left the scene. Dropouts found a life filled with a reasonable amount of happiness and productivity awaiting them.

Not so today—we live and teach in a world where children occupy a more central position. It is no longer seen as the child's fault if he ignores the teacher, distracts others, is destructive, fights, withdraws, or shows other behavior not suited to the traditional classroom. No longer able to gain control over students with a few well-directed punishments, the teacher often feels oppressed by the necessity to be "all things to all children." Having been taught that they must understand each child to lead him profitably through the school experience, teachers are confused and bewildered by the enormity of the task. When they look around for possible help of a tangible nature, they find the same tools and facilities that were there before, gaudier and in more abundance, but still of very limited usefulness. When today's teachers take a careful look at students, as no teachers before have dared to do, they find an incomprehensible mass of behaviors seeming to emerge from all possible kinds of desires and needs. When they listen and observe, they hear and see comments and behaviors like these:[1]

---

1. These are comments selected from more than two hundred that were heard and recorded on one given day by forty teachers.

"The reason I don't get good grades in math is I don't like it."

"Why should I study the life cycle of the moth? I want to be an automobile mechanic."

"The teacher doesn't care. He never gives back our papers. Why should I work when I don't know how I'm doing?"

"What kind of grade do I have to make to get an "E" (excellent) on my next report card?"

"I don't care if I get suspended. I don't want to go to school any way."

"I never thought you could do so much with a typewriter!"

"I want to transfer out of this class. I don't like it."

"Can we take the project home and work on it?"

"Do we *have* to do this?"

"This book is too hard. It doesn't even give the spelling list. I don't know what I'm supposed to study."

"Why should I read the book for the test — he never takes anything out of it anyway?"

After receiving several failing grades, a pupil raised his hand and said "When I drop out of school, I'll come back to see you."

"I can't wait for art tomorrow. We're going to use oil paints."

"I've got to practice my jump shot. They're choosing the basketball team next week."

"May I come to the after school class to learn these fractions?"

Is it any wonder that teachers consistently report that they find it difficult to perform with confidence the act of motivating students? They seem to encounter at least two problems. Overt behaviors of students often are directed toward goals and purposes that are not in the main theme of the classroom experience as the teacher sees it. And teachers are saying, also, that when behavior diverges, they cannot come up with a technique that will set everyone on the pathway thought to be the one they should follow. These two conditions are at the heart of many other problems and difficulties for teachers and for students.

Courses in preparation for entering teaching generally have failed to help teachers anticipate the variety of motivational conditions of their students. Instead, a confused body of literature touching upon two or three contradicting theories of motivation has been exposed for whatever value it might hold. And when a teacher trainee has sought among theory and research for an understanding of student motivation, he has found very little to be of use to him.

Traditionally, theories of motivation are built upon the nature and interrelatedness of underlying forces and are not concerned with the specific behaviors observable to the teacher. Hilgard (1964) has very skillfully pointed out that there is no direct relationship between theory and application. Research in psychology is not often helpful in bridging this gap. Instead of selecting the complex atmosphere of classrooms filled with human subjects, the researching psychologist has shown a distinct preference for the rat in a simple maze. Hence, we know a lot about the simple behavior of subhumans while the behavior of children in classroom learning situations remains unexplored.

Add to this theoretical dilemma the confusions teachers encounter when they read education writers who speak of motivation. It is common to find statements pointing out the absolute necessity for specific motivation to exist before learning will occur. The words of McNally and Passow (1960) are typical.

> In a real sense, it can be said that children learn only that which they want to learn. We have far to go in devising a curriculum and method consonant with this fact. How best can we capitalize the needs and interests that children bring with them to school? (p. 16)

This viewpoint has been with us for several generations, and its effect upon teaching and curriculum has been, at most, superficial. Teachers must keep teaching. They can't stop long enough to find the students' motives and particular interests. And if they knew the individual needs and peculiarities, the means to take them into account might be inappropriate in a large-group teaching situation.

Recently, however, a new viewpoint has come into educational discussions. This position is stated clearly by Ausubel (1963).

> Frequently, the best way of motivating an unmotivated pupil is to ignore his motivational state for the time being and concentrate on teaching him as effectively as possible. Much to his surprise and to his teacher's, he will learn despite his lack of motivation; and from the satisfaction of learning, he will characteristically develop the motivation to learn more (p. 462).

While this seems to place motivation in a secondary role in learning, it actually does not. It simply recognizes that the ingredient of a deep, underlying drive to learn may not be an absolute necessity as has been thought in the past. It implies, in effect, that motivation, absent in the beginning, may be created from the teaching process and built upon by successful experience.

Teachers have long been told that they must know and understand their students in order to teach them effectively. And yet, based solely upon their past performances, they know that effective teaching is possible despite lack of knowledge and understanding of the student. Rudolph Dreikurs (1968) asks "Is it possible to get along with children and to guide them without insight into their psychological dynamics, their motivation?" (p. 36) He goes on to say that the answer to his question is "yes." Those who persist in the viewpoint that the child's own desires, needs, and interests, must determine what he learns are proposing impossible demands on the teacher and the school. If children truly have as many motives as they appear to have, how can a teacher be expected to know them all? Understanding their motives is even more demanding. Indeed, a team of psychiatrists and psychologists with all their knowledge and techniques would find it impossible to understand thirty children and have any time left over to handle the teaching chores. If we suppose that such understanding is possible, then we immediately face another complex problem. How do all of children's needs and interests translate into a school program? McNally and Passow point out that we are a long way from accomplishing this feat. And aren't needs and interests likely to change from group to group? Only a computer able to make rapid decisions about curriculum, instruction, and the like could handle such a mammoth task, and then only if someone knew how to program it. The cold, hard fact is that psychologists and education professors, at this point in time, do not possess the knowledge and skill to solve the problem. In the meantime, children present ever more challenging differences, social conflict mounts, and the school faces new problems daily. Unless we are prepared to abandon the educational enterprise, we must agree with Dreikurs that it is possible to teach children effectively without understanding everything about them.

At this point, several questions might reasonably be asked. Has all the thought and research into motivation been a waste when examined from the viewpoint of the teacher? What, if anything, ought a teacher to know about motivational theory? How does a teacher go about his job without giving immediate attention to the motivational states of students? Is there research evidence to support instructional technology in the classroom? The remainder of this book is devoted to bringing before teachers already on the job and those preparing to teach what the writer sees as realistic answers to these questions.

A Workable Point of View

It is easy to find agreement that education has lacked a generally acceptable point of view about motivation. The science of psychology has provided a large accumulation of fact and theory about general motives of behavior. Teaching, however, is an art and cannot successfully make direct applications of laboratory findings to classroom conditions. There must be an intermediate step wherein scientific principles are translated into practices and procedures for teachers to use. In general, this translation has not occurred in matters pertaining to motivation. Instead, teachers have been left on their own to translate whatever science of human behavior they have learned into successful practice.

For the classroom teacher, a workable approach to motivation should have two components. First, the teacher should know and be able to apply in daily teaching those practices which have been found to be effective in motivating learning in the vast majority of students. Those students who do not respond to generally successful practices require the teacher to call upon a second resource, namely, a knowledge of the psychology of individual behavior. From a reservoir of psychological information about individual motivation, the teacher constructs and applies learning experiences to motivate the reluctant learner. Under ideal circumstances, the individual moves from the need for special treatment to the readiness to respond to those techniques which are effective with general student groups.

This book is an attempt to provide a source to improve a teacher's understanding of the motivation of all children. Also, there are principles discussed for the purpose of creating for the teacher a posture from which effective actions will emerge to influence children to modify their own behavior. The role of the teacher is viewed as that of stimulator of student behavior which constitutes the learning experience. Motivation for school learning is a learning in itself. As such, it can be created out of the proper experiences. In turn, teachers can nurture and cause to grow stronger the desire to learn.

Understanding Motivational Literature

A major problem of communication immediately confronts the teacher who seeks to explore the research and writing concerning motivation. Language used to discuss the topic is faulty. Concise meanings and common agreement are difficult to find. Psychologists, who are ever so careful in planning and conducting their experiments, are often content to describe their findings in language so obscure that the meanings are hidden. Terms such as *motivation, motive, drive, need,* and *goal* are all used interchangeably in one place or another. Only from the context can a term be understood.

Motivation has been defined in a variety of ways. Despite variations from writer to writer, it is common that three qualities are included in most definitions: (1) it is a presumed internal force, (2) that energizes for action, and (3) determines the direction of that action. The most common use of the word *motivation* is as a generic term to designate a topic for discussion, an area for research and study, or to refer to the three underlying factors of behavior pointed out above. As a general term, it may take on meanings as a particular writer may choose. In this book, it will refer to a general body of content including energizing, organizing, directing, and satisfying elements of behavior. It will be considered as a specific only when preceded by an identifying term, for example, achievement-motivation, affiliation-motivation.

Use of the term *motive* is quite confusing in the literature of psychology and education. Often, it is carelessly substituted for *motivation,* but normally, it is used to designate a single state or condition constituting the cause of a given behavior. It is meant to answer the question, "Why does an organism behave in a given way?" Ambiguity is raised by the term because it has meanings in ordinary language which, when applied in a psychology context, create problems of understanding. Peters (1960) points out that there are many answers to the question "Why?", but that not all of them could be classed as *motives.* Let us ask the question, "Why did John study algebra tonight?" Are we asking why John, of all people, would study algebra tonight? Are we questioning his choice of a subject to study? Or, do we want to know why he chose tonight to study when he might have gone to the school dance? *Motive* carries a connotation of purpose which defines what a given action is meant to accomplish for the individual. Thus, a psychologist describing the behavior of subhumans should be careful in his use of the term. *Motive* is used in this discussion to designate the purpose or desired outcome of a behavior.

Drive is a term commonly used in the literature of motivation. Initially, its meaning came from ordinary language. It was used to describe the actuating, moving functions of motivation. Later, it came to designate the name of such primary need conditions as sex, hunger, thirst, and so forth. Primary drives were thought to spawn secondary drives by means never clearly described. Secondary needs or drives were defined as second-order deficiencies which arise while the organism is in the act of satisfying primary or survival needs. To understand the literature of motivation, readers must be aware that the term *drive* may refer either to energy converted to action or to a state of need of primary or secondary origin.

A *goal* is a point to be attained by an individual's actions. The nature of the goal can be determined by someone else and can be communicated to the learner with varying degrees of forcefulness and persuasion. Individual learners set their own goals, also. Both conditions are discussed later.

Reinforcement is a term often used in discussions of learning and motivation. It refers to a "state of affairs" which increases the probability that the behavior with which it is associated will be repeated. The most common misunderstanding occurs because of confusion with the term *reinforcer.* Praise, a pat on the back, a nasty remark, and a hostile glance all are reinforcers. The effect they help to create in the learner is called reinforcement. Positive reinforcement, a satisfying condition, can result from the application of a positive reinforcer or from the witholding of a negative reinforcer. Negative reinforcement, an annoying condition, can be created by applying a negative (noxious) reinforcer or by witholding a positive reinforcer. Later discussion relating to teacher behavior includes references to all these conditions and their probable influence upon student motivation.

2

Early Theory and
Research in Motivation

Recorded history shows us the persistent efforts of man to account for his own actions. Not content just to let his behavior speak for itself, he long ago began to search for the causes and purposes he somehow knew were there. In the course of examining and explaining human actions, many patterns and perspectives have been applied. Because history deals with the past and contains man's mistakes along with his successes, people have often regarded it as being of no practical value in coping with the affairs of the present. Contemporary views of motivation, nevertheless, must stand in perspective against earlier viewpoints and must be interpreted in terms of knowledge that man has accumulated about himself in the past. For these reasons, a brief account of the main advances in explaining motivation is presented in this chapter. Supporting and opposing arguments, as well as descriptions of tangential pursuits, must be ignored for the sake of space and purpose. It is a biased account, however, because of the author's opinions concerning the usefulness of certain theoretical positions when applied in teaching.

Instincts

Almost any teacher today, if told that a student did something "instinctively," would discount the comment or point out that instincts were discarded long ago. There was a time prior to and during World War I when instinct theory flourished in psychology and education. Common behavior for which no specific learning could be identified was explained by saying it was innate.

In 1890, William James, in his *The Principles of Psychology,* defined instinct as a capability to act so as to bring about a certain outcome, without foreseeing that outcome, and without having been taught that particular capability. He believed that man possessed many

8

instincts, more, in fact, than any other animal. Exhaustive lists of instincts began to appear, and semantic problems prevented the clearing up of conflicts and overlaps among the lists. Eventually, it became apparent that *instinct* was being used to refer to two different kinds of phenomena. Sometimes it was used to refer to behaviors such as fighting, sucking, crying, imitation, and locomotion. In other instances, the term was applied to conditions like fear, love, jealousy, hunger, and sex. Arguments developed over the extent to which instincts could be modified by habit. Out of these conditions, two rather divergent patterns among psychologists seem to have emerged. One group developed the study of behavior formation (learning). Among them, names like Pavlov, Watson, and Thorndike are recognized as early leaders. Their concern about human motivation was minimal, but they sought to explain how habits form out of experiences. Another group began to explore the conditions which appeared to energize behavior, and their interest obviously related more closely to motivation.

Classification of a wide variety of behaviors as innate and resistant to easy modification put them conveniently outside the domain of the school and its responsibility. More than that, it gave the school a mode of operation, a focus. Behaviors that were viewed as favorable to the school and to the society of the time were considered either as behaviors to be learned (and thus not instincts) or as instincts to be utilized and allowed to continue. Bothersome and unfavorable behaviors were likely to be seen as instincts—natural and unlearned. Only one method of dealing with undesirable behavior was practiced. Such behavior was punished and made to disappear. Thus, the focus of the school was very early given to punishment and thwarting, with little or no concern for creating conditions wherein students could learn to change their behavior so as to allow personal expression while, at the same time, meeting standards of acceptability. Unfortunately, this focus has been extremely resistant to change despite our willingness to discard instinct as a theory of behavior causation.

Primary Drives and Homeostasis

A beginning for the movement toward *drive* as the central concept of motivation can be found in the work of Robert Woodworth. He selected the simple machine as his model for thinking about human behavior and conceived of actions as mechanisms. Of course, mechanisms must be set in motion by some source of energy. Woodworth was the first to speak of urges or conditions of deficiency, like hunger and thirst, as drives or energizers of behavior (Hall 1961).

Later, Cannon (1932) made an enormous impact upon psychology with his statement which attempted to explain how drives function to energize behavior. He had discovered that when conditions of hunger were experienced by the body, stomach contractions began and that they persisted until food ingestion took place. Stomach contractions were accompanied by persistent and tormenting stimuli, a form of internal pain. Cannon interpreted this pain as the body's way of insuring that its survival needs would be satisfied. The term *homeostasis* was proposed as a name for the tendency of the body to maintain a relatively constant state of equilibrium in its many physiological systems. Thus, the primary drive concept came into being, characterized by conditions of biological need for survival. It has been accepted that the homeostatic process produces the regulatory conditions to insure that drives will result in action.

It was some time later that the concept of motivation as *drive reduction* was articulated. In the writings of Clark Hull (1943) and Miller and Dollard (1941), we find a model of learning with drive as a principal component. Hull postulated that the drive initiated behaviors and that the behavior was goal-directed, seeking something (reward) that would reduce the drive. Many experiments have shown that learning occurs when food and water are given to hungry or thirsty animals. These creatures tend to repeat the behavior associated with getting the reward, and the reward tends to reduce the animals' goal-seeking activity. Thus it has been demonstrated beyond any doubt that primary drives of animals can energize them to seek satisfaction and that satisfaction is drive-reducing in nature. This model of motivation, however, may not be adequate to explain all the conditions of human learning, as we shall see in later discussions.

Although the primary drive concept and drive reduction theory have made an immense impact upon psychology, the effect in the home and in the school has been quite limited. Psychologists turned to the animal in the laboratory and found the manipulation of hunger and thirst conditions to be quite satisfactory as their means for energizing and controlling learning. At home, children experience only a short period of time when deep concern for primary needs is uppermost in their lives. In infancy, the body adjusts to a feeding schedule rather quickly, and only rarely does the child experience extreme hunger or thirst after the period of early infancy. Parent and child interactions seldom have their principal focus upon the satisfaction of immediate body needs. When the child has adequate care as a routine part of his life experience, it is taken for granted and becomes an important but regular part of daily living. Since parents seldom manipulate the primary biological needs (food, water, warmth, etc.) in order to direct behavior, it is not readily apparent how such needs could be the basis for all motivation.

It is next to impossible to see a child of school age experiencing exclusively a primary drive condition. Ordinarily, many social learnings have come into his behavior to complicate the motivational scheme. The school has never been seen as a place for learning how to satisfy primary drives. Rewards and punishments have been similar to those received by the child at home. Children in school sometimes show behaviors which appear to be associated with unsatisfied primary needs, hunger and sex, in particular. In such cases, the need seems to interfere with, rather than motivate, the behaviors teachers want to encourage. We know very little about the effects of prolonged deprivation of survival needs upon learning of academic material. Certainly, we know nothing about methods to overcome the residuals of such conditions, and we are ignorant of the method whereby conflicting drives are resolved. Other problems associated with the concept of primary drives are discussed in the following chapter where more recent research and theory are examined.

Secondary Drives

Not satisfied with primary drives as explanations of human behavior, psychologists moved quickly into more complex conditions. Introduction of the idea of secondary drives was the contribution of E. C. Tolman who wanted to describe more of human behavior under the drive concept. First-order drives, appetites and aversions, were thought to be the foundation of all behavior by providing the organism with ultimate approach-avoidance demands and some direction in their satisfaction. In his *Purposive Behavior in Animals and Men*, Tolman (1932) suggests that certain ancillary drives of a second order are evident in man and in other higher animals. He lists curiosity, gregariousness, self-assertion, self-abasement, and imitativeness as a tentative list of secondary drives. He thought of them as aversions aroused by threatening external conditions. By some means not clear to Tolman, these second-order drives were described as springing from the circumstances surrounding an individual's attempt to satisfy his primary needs.

A suggestion by Allport (1937) that needs (*motives,* as he named them) become "functionally autonomous" from their sources gained considerable attention.

> Each motive has a definite point of origin which may possibly lie in instincts, or, more likely, in the organic tensions of infancy. Chronologically speaking, all adult purposes can be traced back to these seed-forms in infancy, but as the individual matures the tie is broken. Whatever bond remains is historical, not functional (p. 143).

Secondary drives, he suggested, are the result of certain behaviors which were instrumental in acquiring satisfaction for primary needs.

After continued use, these instrumental behaviors acquire autonomy and generalize (spread) to new situations. Thus they are perpetuated into later life. Since the antecedent conditions are no longer evident, Allport suggests that motivation should be studied in its contemporary, not in its earlier structure. This seems to tell us to look for the current gains a behavior is bringing for the student. A behavior such as ignoring the teacher may initially emerge as a means of avoiding a circumstance likely to lead to failure. However, if this behavior somehow causes the student to gain attention from his peers, he may continue to ignore the teacher for the purpose of getting social recognition. Allport was speaking of larger components of behavior, but his thoughts seem to be applicable to the acquisition of any new behavior. That we should seek the purposes of behavior rather than its causes is the point of real significance in Allport's statement.

Basic Needs

Following Allport's statement on "functional autonomy," a major change took place in psychology. A concern for the mental hygiene of individuals had grown to sufficient proportions in the total profession that its influence began to be evident. While laboratory psychologists continued to refer to primary and secondary drives, those who were more interested in individual behavior began to use the term *basic need*. Both survival needs and acquired needs were listed as basic. A need was considered to be basic if it suited either or both of the following conditions: (1) it was found to exist in the population at large (a common need); and (2) it related to the acquisition of a goal of significant importance in physical or psychological good health. Thus, the concept of basic need included both innate and acquired needs.

For the earliest statement of real consequence in the matter of basic need, we must turn to Murray (1938). Adhering to the two-fold approach to classification of need, he referred to two principal types: (1) primary (viscerogenic) needs; and (2) secondary (psychogenic) needs. Viscerogenic needs are brought about by periodic bodily events like hunger, thirst, bowel and bladder distention, and the like. Murray (1938) described psychogenic needs as being brought about by strong, prevalent tensions stimulated by certain environmental conditions or images representing such conditions. He listed eleven viscerogenic and twenty-six psychogenic needs. Since his terms often require an explanation, the list is not shown here, but interested readers should consult his original work. From his long list of psychogenic needs, only two have received extensive research scrutiny—need for achievement and need for affiliation. They will be discussed later.

Individuals are seen to be unique in their ways of displaying particular needs and to show changes in their need patterns from time to time. Basic needs are observed as learned-reaction systems or behaviors that can be distinguished by a common type of content. Examples found in most lists of needs are the need to be aggressive, to play, to be accepted, to be recognized, to achieve, and to defend oneself. A need is assumed to be latent or dormant in the personality until a stimulating condition causes it to be aroused. Then, when it has received adequate satisfaction, it becomes less evident in the overall pattern of behavior of the individual. Many of the earlier attributes of homeostasis as they applied to energizing the organism to seek satisfaction for primary (viscerogenic) needs have been applied to psychogenic needs as well. A general state of well-being or equilibrium is assumed to be sought by healthy people. When this state is threatened by deprivation of one or more of its basic psychological needs, behavior aimed at righting the balance is initiated.

Murray's work initiated a vigorous effort to name a need for almost any identifiable act of human behavior. It had been widely accepted that "all behavior is motivated." Consistent with this viewpoint, the simplest way of interpreting behavior was to assume that if an individual did something, he had a need to do it. This position brought about lists of needs extending to as many as forty (Combs 1946). It became difficult to see much usefulness or meaning in the confusion that developed. Semantic problems, overlaps, and omissions resulted in an endless maze of confusion. Nevertheless, the impact of the basic needs concept in psychology and education remains evident even today.

Hierarchy of Needs

A different approach to the concept of need is proposed by Maslow (1943, 1954). Out of his clinical and experimental knowledge, he extracted six categories of need. Observation led him to conclude that these exist in a hierarchical order—that when needs at one level are satisfied, an individual moves to the next higher level to seek gratification. Maslow's categories are as follows:

(1) **Physiological**
(2) **Safety**
(3) **Belongingness or love**
(4) **Esteem**
(5) **Self-actualization**
(6) **Aesthetic**

In fairness to his concept, it must be said that Maslow recognized that exceptions could exist—that an individual could appear to skip over certain levels or to regress to a lower level of need gratification. For a thorough description and explanation of his viewpoint, the reader is referred to Maslow's works cited above.

Later, Maslow (1955) further differentiated his hierarchy into two categories: deficiency motivation and growth motivation. He observed that healthy individuals are people who have achieved sufficient satisfaction of their needs for safety, belongingness, love, respect, and self-esteem. Essentially, they are people who are functioning at the self-actualizing level of the hierarchy. Unhealthy individuals, then, are those whose lives are characterized by the search for gratification of their deficiencies in the levels of the hierarchy below self-actualization. Maslow speaks of them as deficiency motivated, whereas, those who are functioning at the self-actualizing level are seen as growth motivated.

Building upon the concept of the need for self-actualization, Maslow observes that healthy children enjoy growing, and that they enjoy learning new behaviors and gaining capability to master their environment. Self-actualization, as he defines it, includes continual development of potentials, fulfillment of desires and undertakings, realization of one's own intrinsic character, and a dynamic trend toward functional wholeness.

Another important distinction is made between deficiency and growth motivation. In general, needs and drives are viewed as aversive, irritating, unpleasant states to be reduced by gratification. For Maslow, this describes deficiency motivation. Growth, or self-actualizing motivation, does not fit this model. Satisfaction brings the desire for more gratification, and the growth-motivated person seeks to build upon his level of achievement rather than to find satisfaction at a given point and cease his strivings. Growth motivation, as a concept, seems to be closely related to what many others speak of as intrinsic motivation, a topic for later discussion.

One Basic Human Need

In 1949, Snygg and Combs in their book, *Individual Behavior*, introduced a new viewpoint in psychology, and with it, a new concept of need. Their work resulted from dissatisfaction with several aspects of psychology at the time. The "external approach," observing and testing subjects in order to predict their behavior, was felt to be inadequate when applied to individuals. While group norms were sufficient to aid the scientist in the development of his theories, they seldom seemed to relate to a particular person in a given situation. What seemed to be necessary was a system or approach that could be applied to any individual, above or below the average, in order to better understand his behavior. The personal or phenomenological approach was their solution to the problem.

Individual psychology is built upon a concept of the "phenomenal field." It is defined as ". . . the entire universe, including himself, as it is experienced by the individual at the instant of action" (Snygg and Combs 1949, p. 15). They go on to say that it is simply the unique, naïve, everyday situation of the individual and his surroundings that he takes as his own reality. How an individual behaves is determined, not by what others experience, but by what he as a unique organism perceives as the situation and his relationship within it.

In this frame of reference, only one basic need is seen as important —"the preservation and enhancement of the phenomenal self" (Snygg and Combs p. 58). Whatever one does, it has a purpose—to maintain or improve one's circumstance as his individual perception of himself and his personal world dictates. When behavior is observed, it often seems to be strange and senseless. To the individual himself, the behavior has order and meaning in his own world. How often have we heard or said the words, "I know it seems strange to you but . . ."? Only by getting to know an individual quite well can an observer have a good understanding of his behavior. When this is accomplished, it begins to make sense and may, in fact, seem wise.

The phenomenological viewpoint has been influential in clinical and counseling psychology. It has not, however, had the impact in education that it should. Teachers would find this way of interpreting behavior useful. It does not require one to search all the complex of needs for the one or more that are causing a particular behavior. Instead, the teacher's attention and search is directed toward purposes. What is the purpose of the behavior—what is it meant to accomplish? Purposes are much easier to infer than are needs, and they are easier to understand in terms of an individual and a situation. For those who wish to read further into this topic, Snygg and Combs (1949) and Dreikurs (1968) are helpful.

Attitudes and Interests

When writing about motivation, many authors give little, if any, consideration to attitudes and interests. One has only to listen to the language of teachers, though, to realize how often they call upon these terms when they conceptualize student behavior. A teacher might say, "John has a negative attitude toward everything related to studying," or "Mary certainly is interested in insects, especially butterflies," or even, "Bill puts honesty above everything." These are convenient ways of expressing the particular elements of personality which are more important than others in directing behavior. Thus, whereas needs are accepted as stimulating behavior, attitudes, interests, and values tend to shape actions in relationship to specific objects and goals. This distinction has not been clear in all instances, as shown in the words of Walker (1964). Speaking as a member of the Nebraska Symposium on Motivation, he said, "Thus, innate biological motives, acquired human motives, sets, attitudes, and traits may be regarded as alike in being readiness to respond selectively to limited classes of stimuli or to select limited classes of events by an identical mechanism" (p. 90). He goes on to say that "motives such as need for achievement and attitudes are indistinguishable in that both are acquired, both are enduring, but both are subject to modification."

Attitudes: Speaking of an attitude, Allport (1935) defined it as a "mental and neural state of readiness, organized through experience, exerting a directive or dynamic influence upon the individual response to all objects with which it is related" (p. 810). Others have regarded attitudes as "emotional stereotypes" and have described them as having either three or four characteristics (Stagner 1948; Russell 1959):

(1) an object, considered to be the intellectual or cognitive description of a thing or an experience;

(2) a direction, the pleasantness or unpleasantness associated with the object;

(3) an intensity, the amount of excitement or arousal released by the object;

(4) an extensity, the extent to which the feeling tone is generalized or spread to surrounding objects.

An example of a predisposing characteristic considered to be very important in school is a child's attitude toward authority figures. This attitude is assumed to develop from emotional experiences with parents or parent substitutes and to be shaped by subsequent interactions with teachers, policemen, and others in ascendance positions. In a study of 400 students and their parents, Itkin (1955) found a strong relationship between the attitudes of both boys and girls toward authority figures and the extent of the father's acceptance or rejection of the child in early life. Relationships with adults are found, also, to be strongly influenced by the painful and distressing experiences of loss of a mother figure in the period prior to three years of age (Spitz 1951; Ribble 1944; Roudinesco 1952). In a study of 384 children five and six years of age, Koch (1955) found three conditions in the mother-child relationship to have a strong influence upon attitudes toward the teacher:

(1) the extent of satisfying experiences with mother,

(2) mother's expectations of the child,

(3) attitudes of the mother toward the siblings.

An early concern is evident in determining how children form their attitudes toward other children. In particular, it is noted that attitudes among white children toward blacks has received considerable attention. Horowitz and Horowitz (1938) reported that, characteristically, young children show no particular attitude in early life but acquire an attitude from what they are told and from experiences with their parents. Blake and Dennis (1943) point out much the same basis for racial attitudes and add that first the child acquires an unfavorable attitude which makes him unwilling to look for "good" traits. They say, further, that "with increased age and experience, the child gradually learns to apply adult stereotypes, a few of which are complimentary." Naturally, these two early research studies are devoted to the genesis of negative attitudes which were more prevalent then. It is probable, however, that positive attitudes of whites toward blacks and the attitudes of blacks toward whites form in this way, also.

There was an early concern to discover the genesis of attitudes of nonconformity. General agreement is found in Flügel (1926), Lasswell (1930), Krout and Stagner (1939), and Stagner (1944) that radical attitudes develop from reactions to children's feelings of rejection by their parents. These writers found in their studies that a substantial proportion of radicals seemed to be rebelling against the values held by the parents and by society in general. However, a study reported by Newcomb (1943) points out that the environment has a strong influence upon conformity. Children may come from either liberal or conservative homes and be influenced by their peers to change in surroundings different from their homes. Teachers today encounter attitudes of nonconformity and are often frustrated by them. Research done in an earlier era may not be sufficient to aid in understanding students of today, and the teacher may have to seek answers in contemporary literature.

Level of aspiration is a special case of attitude—special because of the attention it has received among those interested in motivation. Kurt Lewin is credited with the first development of the concept (Travers 1967), but an early definition by Gardner (1940) is offered here. After reviewing many uses of the term, Gardner concluded: "There is, then, one and only one meaning to the term *level of aspiration:* it can only refer to a quantitative indication which an individual makes concerning his future performance in an activity" (p. 66). One of the earliest significant studies of aspirations was conducted by Jueknat (1937) using 500 school children divided into three groups based on their performance of school tasks. Children in the highest achievement group had the highest aspirations, and those in the middle achievement group had moderate aspirations. Children in the low achievement group divided, with some having high and others having low aspirations. The same findings were reported soon thereafter by Sears (1940) who found that unsuccessful ten- and twelve-year-olds set either low or high goals. The implication of this finding may be that children who fail to achieve either give up or set unrealistically high goals out of a desire to improve or to protect their own concepts of self. Research has consistently reported that aspirations are a function of success in previous tasks (Sears 1940; Gardner 1940; Child and Whiting 1949; Steisel and Cohen 1951). Teachers who seek to raise the level of aspiration of children who are failing should take note that the only effective means appears to be a series of successful experiences.

Attitudes, while they are relatively resistant, appear to be subject to change. The influence of a particular teacher, another child, an event, academic learning, and the extracurricular program of the school can be effective in the modification of attitudes. Psychodrama has been shown to be an effective technique for attitudinal change in children as young as nursery school and kindergarten age. Lippitt and Clancy (1954) demonstrated that children of this age changed from destructive to constructive and creative as the result of a period of psychodrama.

Some attitudes, however, resist change unless very potent approaches are employed. Racial attitudes have been found to persist despite close contact with children of other races. Mussen (1950) found that casual contact, made possible through school camping, did not insure a decrease in prejudice. Sister Mary Ita (1950) expressed the idea that strongly emotional techniques may succeed better because prejudices have a strong emotional component. The effect of a permissive classroom atmosphere upon attitude changes has been reported by Metcalf (1950) and Elliott and Moustakas (1951), among others. Catharsis, the release of stored-up feeling, takes place more readily in an atmosphere free from threat. Insight is most likely to occur when several differing viewpoints are expressed freely. Together, these two conditions have been found to have a significant impact upon feelings and attitudes. Ordinary classroom discussions of topics such as juvenile delinquency do not have noticeable direct influences upon attitudes (Lagey 1956; Russell 1959).

Statements and findings relative to attitudes have been quite influential in education. The language has been, from the beginning, quite understandable for teachers, and there has been a consistent opinion that attitudes are subject to the teacher's influence where some other elements of motivation seem farther removed. Unfortunately, very little help has been given the teacher to learn how to develop certain attitudinal characteristics and to modify existing ones. In general, the techniques teachers have used tend to lack the intense impact and prolonged exposure ordinarily required for significant changes to occur.

Interests: Interests, like attitudes, have held a place in discussions of motivation for a long time. The term has undergone a slight change since it was defined by William James (1890) as a form of attention or awareness that helps man to produce meaning out of the mass of his experiences. Since then, the likes, dislikes, and preoccupations evidenced by both speech and action have been called interests. They have been assessed and thereby defined in three ways:

(1) **inferred from what a person does and seems to enjoy (manifest interest);**

(2) **assessed from questions asking what activities are liked and disliked (expressed interests); and**

(3) **measured by placing various activities against each other and asking persons to select one or the other (inventoried interests).**

As one might expect, a person's interests may vary considerably, depending upon which method is used to learn about them (Berdie 1955). For this reason, the research relating to interest must be examined carefully to know its meaning. Space must limit us to a very brief review of the subject, and the vast literature must be left to the reader to examine for himself.

Longitudinal studies have revealed some of the characteristics of interests as they exist in children. Among the few authors who have sought to trace interest from childhood on is Tyler (1951, 1955). In a study of 115 children in kindergarten and first grade, she was able to find four kinds of interest patterns:

(1) **active outdoor play,**
(2) **play with toys outdoors,**
(3) **paper and pencil activity,**
(4) **working with adults.**

Interests at this stage of development, Tyler found, were already dividing along sex lines. Later, in a study of fourth grade children, an even stronger relationship with sex role was observed. Boys rejected things associated with being a sissy and with female work. Girls disliked physical activity, aggression, and other things deemed out of order for females. Later, of course, the same children may find themselves changing to a temporary interest in the very things they had rejected at an earlier period. In an extensive study of 2,234 children in grades four through eight, Kaufman (1955) found several interesting characteristics of the age group studied:

1. Interest increased for organized games as children grew older.

2. Strong biological concerns were evident.

3. Boys were more interested in science and mathematics, whereas girls liked language arts and social studies better.

4. Interest in heterosexual group activities grew during this period.

5. Interest in gang activities was strongest for boys at ten-twelve years and for girls at twelve-thirteen years of age.

Other studies of significance have served to describe interests and to relate them to other aspects of the individual. One of the most significant studies of the period was done by Jersild and Tasch (1949). Their survey included more than 3,000 children in many communities over the country. Among their many findings are these:

1. Children show a decided interest in interpersonal relationships at all ages.

2. There is a tendency to relate their interests to their own self-concepts.

3. In early grades especially, a high interest is shown in receiving gifts.

4. Teachers seem to have an influence upon interests, as shown by differences between schools and classes.

5. Interests are influenced by learning opportunities.

6. Increasing age brings more interest in self-improvement, self-understanding, and understanding of others.

7. As children grow older, they see the school as less and less related to their personal goals, and they have a decreasing interest in school.

8. The subject viewed most unfavorably was social studies.

9. Interests expressed by children are not related to needs of the child.

Interests have been grouped into several categories. The listing given the most attention has been the classifications by Super (1957). He divided interests into:

(1) scientific interest, which involves the comprehension of biological and physical processes and the desire to use such knowledge in practical matters;

(2) technical or material interest, stressing mastery and application rather than theory and understanding;

(3) social welfare interest, which is a concern for people for their own sake;

(4) systematic or business detail interest, which focuses upon rules, controls, neatness, and orderliness;

(5) business contact interest, which means dealing with others as a means to an end, with personal gain as the most frequent goal;

(6) literary interest, which includes interest in words and their use to get and to express ideas or to influence others; and

(7) music and artistic interests, ranging from performance to appreciation.

Perhaps Super (1949) best summarizes the thoughts of most writers who have shown concern as to how interests develop when he says:

> Interests are the product of interaction between inherited aptitudes and endocrine factors, on the one hand, and opportunity and social

evaluation on the other. Some of the things a person does will bring him the satisfaction of mastery or the approval of his companions, and result in interests. Some of the things his associates do appeal to him and, through identification, he patterns his actions and his interests after them; if he fits the pattern reasonably well he remains in it, but if not, he must seek another identification and develop another self-concept and interest pattern (p. 406).

Anne Roe (1957) suggests many of the same conclusions but attempts to deal with the motivational aspects of interest in a deeper vein. She feels that psychic energy in early life gets directed into patterns determined by satisfactions and frustrations. Needs satisfied as they appear do not seem to become deep and strong motivators, whereas needs which receive delayed but eventual satisfaction do become strong motivators. Emotional situations in the home help to develop certain specific interests. In homes where there is overprotection of the child, belongingness, love, and esteem often are conditional upon being dependent and upon conforming to parental demands. In such a climate, the child is likely to develop interests and behaviors associated with extrinsic rewards and approval from others. If, on the other hand, reasonable gratification of all needs for belongingness, love, and esteem is provided in the home, the child is more likely to show interest in self-improvement for its intrinsic value.

Studies of the extent to which interests predict achievement date back to the early part of the century. Since Thorndike (1917) found a nearly perfect relationship between expressed interest and self-ratings of successful achievement, others have sought to examine interest and achievement. Low, but positive, relationships have consistently been reported (Strong 1949; Berdie 1950; Gowan 1957). Because the measurement of interests of students below age eighteen tends to have doubtful validity and reliability, these studies ordinarily involve college-age groups. Their significance for education below college is meager because of the measurement problem and the time lapse since the research.

Despite many problems, some impact has been felt in education as a result of studies of interest. This has been most evident in the content of children's books and materials. Teachers have shown more concern for the interests of individual children and have made changes in the classroom experience to take special interests into account. One major finding, consistent over the years, has *not* been treated seriously. Boys and girls show major differences in their interests and yet, in the elementary school, programs are kept identical, a fact which may account for many of the motivational problems of boys.

3

Current Theory and Research

Since 1950, a marked change has been noticeable in the kind of topics discussed in the literature of motivation. It is evident, also, that many earlier assumptions have come under criticism since World War II. A long-standing tendency to see all motivation as some form of need reduction has received serious challenge. New pursuits have produced information that leads to a widespread discontent with a motivational theory built entirely upon a concept of primary drives. More important for the teacher is the fact that recent theories and investigations hold greater significance for the classroom. While too much research continues to be done with subhuman animals and not enough with human subjects, a few of the most influential psychologists of our time have turned a portion of their energy toward helping teachers. In this chapter, each of the major recent trends is reviewed, quite briefly, to be sure, and their implications for education are discussed. When information presented in the review of earlier theory and research is coupled with more recent knowledge, a base is formed for the practical suggestions and techniques presented in the remaining chapters.

Arousal

Any statement about motivation, either specific or implied, suggests a condition of arousal. Terms like *activated, energized, stimulated,* and *excited* have been used to describe this condition. Teachers recognize a difference between the overt behaviors of students who are "turned on" and those who are apathetic. We speak of "paying attention" and are quick to recognize when a child is distracted by competing thoughts or extraneous stimulation. These conditions are thought to be related somehow to learning; therefore, we strive to create a setting that will lead to attentiveness, action, and freedom from distractions.

Early in the experimental study of arousal, as Duffy (1966) describes it, a great many physiological evidences were noted. Muscular tension, skin resistance, cardiovascular action, temperature, and other physical conditions were observed to vary from ordinary levels when organisms were aroused. The polygraph (often used as a lie detector) registers such changes when disturbances occur in the autonomic nervous system. Until the report of Maruzzi and Magoun (1949), however, the exact location and manner of functioning of the activating system was only conjecture. They discovered that a column of nerve cells extending through the lower brain produced alertness and attention when it was stimulated with electricity. This region is made up of a network of short fibers and cell bodies with many synapses. Both incoming and outgoing pathways extend from the area and comprise what is called the reticular activating system (RAS). It has been shown that the RAS can be activated by a variety of internal and external stimuli. External inputs through the various senses have an arousal effect, as pointed out by Granit (1955), Jouvet (1957), Funster (1958), and Berlyne (1960).

Sensory inputs travel along two pathways—one leads to the activation center (RAS), and the other to the area of the brain associated with that particular sense organ. In the RAS, the sensory input generates an arousal impulse which is sent over a diffuse network to all areas of the brain. In the sensory area, it is joined by the input coming directly from the sense organ. Together, they produce a heightened sensitivity to stimulation. Berlyne (1960) describes the function of the RAS in these words:

> If a stimulus comes along that is capable of energizing the RAS —a stimulus that is usually intense, like a loud noise or a severe jolt, or one that has special significance, like a faint sound of crying that reaches a sleeping mother—the organism wakes up, and the stimulus begins to affect overt behavior (p. 47).

Discovery that there is a particular brain center for arousal is important. That it can be activated by a variety of internal and external stimuli makes it even more important. But most significant of all is the discovery that, once activated, it continues to interact with the sense organs to increase sensory acuity. Sensations become heightened, and there is an increased awareness as added sensory materials are brought into the process. Any teacher has observed that a seemingly unmotivated student, once his attention is captured by some element of the learning experience, begins to show signs of even more intense interest after continued exposure. Discovery that there is a neurophysical explanation for this circumstance somehow gives us additional confidence that we can have control over it. A stronger case can be made for intensifying our efforts to get and maintain attention. Success in these efforts results in at least a temporary motivation on the part of the learner. While in a state of arousal, if the excitement is not too high, the student is prepared for learning. But the arousal state alone is not sufficient to produce learning. It simply activates. An accompanying effect of increased sensory awareness causes the student to become more acutely aware of the stimuli directing him toward the specifics to be learned.

What stimulus qualities tend to produce arousal in human subjects? Intensity is one quality which has a direct positive effect. Berlyne (1950) reports that a group of subjects, when exposed to a sequence of paired dots of two different light intensities, responded to the brighter one on an average of 13.5 out of sixteen trials. Another series of paired sets, with one of the pair larger than the other, produced similar results. The larger of the pair was responded to on an average of 12.7 times in sixteen trials. In a later set of experiments with visual stimuli, Berlyne (1957) found three qualities to be determining factors in the amount of attention and fascination caused: (1) complex visual patterns were more potent than simple ones; (2) patterns containing a quality of uncertainty (mild ambiguity) were more compelling than were those where the relationships were direct, clear, and simple; and (3) patterns lacking congruity held more attention-getting value than did the ones wherein all elements were compatible and coherent. Addition of chromatic color to visual stimuli, particularly color in the low (red) end of the spectrum, increases the arousal value.

Changing stimuli have more intensity and potential to cause arousal than do those which remain fixed or static. Increases in auditory qualities of both pitch (frequency) and loudness have an arousal quality. Also, the suddenness of the change of either pitch or volume has an alerting effect. Changes in almost any sensory mode produce an increased awareness level (Berlyne 1957), but if the change introduces excessive uncertainty, it may reduce learning efficiency. It has been accepted for many years that moving stimuli have more arousal potential than stationary objects have. Discussing infant perception, Koffka (1935) said that moving stimuli are the first things infants notice. He then built a theoretical proposition that all visual perception has a movement component. Later, Bender (1938), in several studies, secured data supporting this hypothesis. Other aspects of movement, such as its rapidity and direction toward or away from the observer, are qualities relating to the arousal level.

New, novel, and surprising aspects of the environment tend to create arousal both in laboratory animals and in human beings. As early as 1930, Nissen reported that rats would cross an electrified grid to get to explore new objects placed in their cage. Since then, many psychologists have shown that novelty activates subjects to make a response (Kivy, Earl, and Walker 1956; Williams and Kuchta 1957; Fowler 1958). It appears that psychologists have known all along that human beings respond to novelty, but they were quite excited to find similar behavior in rats. Controlled observations of children in novel situations seem to be unavailable, but we have all observed youngsters spending long periods of time investigating machinery, watching construction workers, and playing with new toys or household articles. Isn't it strange that, until we learned that rats do it, too, we gave it little or no consideration in motivation?

Arousal is described as a continuous state going from very deep sleep to conditions of panic. Investigators have searched up and down the continuum for an optimum level where learning is most efficient. Studies of learning during sleep have been reported, and there are reports of learning in conditions of high arousal. Nevertheless, it has come to be well accepted that the optimum level for learning to occur is somewhere in the moderate portion of the arousal curve.

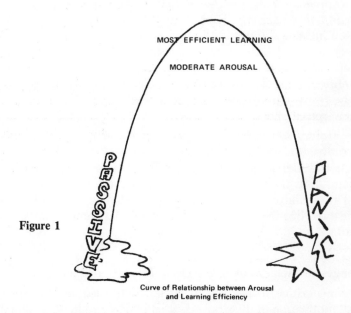

Figure 1

Curve of Relationship between Arousal
and Learning Efficiency

The inverted-U curve represented in Figure 1 has been reported by various investigators (Hebb 1955; Malmo 1959; Berlyne 1960; Fiske and Maddi 1961).

Fiske and Maddi (1961) developed eight propositions concerning optimum arousal level that teachers might find useful. From their eight propositions, four concepts can be extracted and related to behavior in school learning situations:

1. *The level of arousal at any given moment is a function of intensity, novelty, and meaningfulness of all the internal and external stimuli acting on the individual at that moment.* Able to react to many stimuli simultaneously, the arousal system in some way integrates or puts together the impinging stimuli according to the three variables of: intensity (how strong it is), novelty (how much it represents change from previous levels of stimulation), and meaningfulness (how the individual attaches meaning to a stimulus at the particular time).

2. *There are optimum levels of arousal for each kind of task, and the individual behaves in ways designed to maintain the optimum level.* When the impact of all stimuli is too low, the learner does something to turn up the arousal level (turns on the radio while studying). On the other hand, when the impact is too high, something is done to reduce it (pats the foot or chews fingernails to reduce internal tensions during study).

3. *Individuals have sleep-wakefulness cycles which are maintained by the organism's activity.* Each student has a cycle ranging from sleep to wakefulness, and there is a tendency for his behavior to follow patterns consistent with the state of arousal at periods within this cycle. If a student is in a period of high wakefulness and has nothing to occupy his attention, he seeks ways to be stimulated. In periods approaching sleep, he resists stimulation, and the intensity must be raised if it is to have an arousal effect.

4. *Arousal levels have a pleasure-pain or affective component.* When the arousal level exceeds the usual amount for a specific situation, it affects the individual negatively. Affect becomes more pleasurable (less painful) as the arousal level approaches the normal or optimum level. Thus, children who have grown accustomed to high excitement in their everyday lives find the calm, quiet, classroom atmosphere unpleasant.

Challenges to Homeostasis and Drive-Reduction Theories

Serious criticisms have been hurled at the earlier attempt to explain all motivation in the single context of drive-reduction. The drives included among those ordinarily referred to as primary drives have been inadequate to explain exploratory behavior, curiosity, manipulation, and boredom. Homeostasis has been demonstrated to apply in a limited set of physiological need-states but not in others. A consistent failure to show that needs and motives appearing in later life have their origins in the physiological (life-sustaining) needs has cast doubt upon earlier views relating to secondary drives. Observing the extent and validity of these attacks, White (1968) makes the following comment:

> This opens the way for considering in their own right those aspects of animal and human behavior in which stimulation and contact with the environment seem to be sought and welcomed, in which raised tension and even mild excitement seem to be cherished, and in which novelty and variety seem to be enjoyed for their own sake (p. 82).

It may be that teachers have known all along that many motives function in school learning and that most of them would strain the imagination to be seen as being very directly related to the life-sustaining needs of man. They have seen that learning is acquired without extrinsic rewards being given. The child who learns soon develops the need to know more, thereby building a need rather than reducing one. At the same time, teachers certainly have observed that the concept of homeostasis is not sufficient to explain all student behavior. Because most of the earlier thoughts about motivation have not sounded very plausible to teachers anyway, we will not take the space necessary to report the faultfinding. Instead, the reader who wants to know more about critical evaluations is referred to the writings of White (1959), Berlyne (1960), Hunt (1960), and Fowler (1965) who are but a few of those who propose other ideas.

Fear and Anxiety

Pervasive, mysterious, and often avoided, the concepts of fear and anxiety remain aspects of motivation about which teachers ought to know much more. The course of man's history has been closely linked with his fears, and yet, as a topic of study in psychology, fear was scarcely mentioned before World War II. Immediately thereafter, a surge of writing began to fill the void of scientific knowledge.

When we approach this literature, it is, once again, a frustrating experience brought about by a confusion of definitions. Often, no distinct difference is made between fear and anxiety, and many authors are found to use them interchangeably. By others, fear is defined as an aversive emotion brought on by threats to one's physical well-being. This viewpoint then defines anxiety as a somewhat milder aversive feeling generated from real or imaginary threats to the individual's self-esteem (Ausubel and Robinson 1969). Another describes fear as a response to "obvious, objective danger" and anxiety as a response to "conflicting drives, impulses, and unresolved problems " (Jersild 1959). Researchers are accustomed to looking at fear as an acquired secondary drive (Miller 1948; Taylor 1956; Mowrer 1960). Before we proceed, this communication problem ought to be examined to find its importance for teachers.

While there is not space here to show the original writings or even to discuss them, a careful examination reveals clues to the underlying reasons for the jumble of terms. Those who do not bother to differentiate between fear and anxiety customarily deal with intense states of arousal brought about by punishing stimuli applied to animals in the laboratory. When they use the term *fear,* they refer to the high arousal condition created by the punishment (usually shock). Residual fear maintained in the animal and associated with the conditions (secondary reinforcers) under which pain was experienced may be spoken of as *anxiety* if indeed the term is used at all. The term *anxiety* is most common in the writings of mental hygienists who are concerned about human beings. These writers, when they speak of the lingering feeling of impending danger, may use the term *anxiety* and make further differentiations of it to explain its qualities. When mental hygienists speak of *fear,* they are most likely referring to the emotion associated with threat to the physical well-being of the organism.

For the teacher and others whose primary concern is observed behavior and behavioral change, the semantic argument has little importance. Functionally, the difference between fear and anxiety is a matter of the intensity of arousal. The individual's manner of behaving is affected most by the intensity of his feeling and not by whether his behavior results from threat to his physical or his psychological welfare. For that matter, threats of danger seldom involve only the physical or the psychological component, and it is doubtful that the endangered person could make a clear differentiation between the two. In order to respond adequately, he depends more upon the nature of the immediate environment, his past experiences, and the intensity of the arousal at the moment.

Early in the scientific study of learning, Thorndike (1913) made his first statement of the Law of Effect:

> When a modifiable connection between a situation and a response is made and is accompanied or followed by a satisfying state of affairs, that connection's strength is increased: When made and accompanied or followed by an annoying state of affairs, its strength is decreased (p. 4).

By strengthening of a connection, Thorndike meant an increase in the probability that the response will recur. A decrease of strength meant that the response would be less likely to recur. Thus, in his initial statement of the effect of reward and punishment on learning, the two were assumed to have equal and opposite influence. Unable to support his original position, Thorndike later dropped all reference to punishment, and the matter remained dormant for several years. Eventually, when others became interested in a study of the effect produced by punishment, the concept of fear became important as the intervening variable whereby punishment inhibits responses. Mowrer (1960), reviewing the study of punishment, says, ". . . it is now generally conceded that punishment achieves its inhibitory effect, not by the direct stamping out of S–R bonds, but by the intermediation of fear" (p. 25).

Punishment (pain) associated with a given behavior is assumed to leave its trace in the learner. Later, when similar conditions occur, the individual anticipates pain again, and this anticipatory feeling is called fear. Once it has become sufficiently strong, fear can inhibit the response. And, once established, fear can be aroused by the presence of specific conditions which have been present in the original situation. A simple example is a signal light or buzzer occurring simultaneously with an electric shock. With repetition, the light or buzzer alone can produce the fear response. Thus, fear as a response can be attached to signals which retain the potential to inhibit or modify behavior in circumstances not identical with the initial situation.

Sensations of fear are aversive and should be avoided. Two types of avoidance behavior are apparent—*passive avoidance* and *active avoidance.* In the case of passive avoidance, the behavior associated with punishment is simply blocked—the learner just refrains from making the action. In active avoidance situations, he learns that fear can be avoided by doing something to remove himself actively from the threatening conditions. Punishment given at the time, or soon after a response, results in a behavior-correlated fear, and brings about passive avoidance. On the other hand, fear not associated with a specific behavior results in the necessity to do something in order to get relief. It has been clearly established that, in the laboratory, active and passive avoidance can be used to cause animals to do something they do not want to do, and to prevent them from doing what they want to do.

It is not difficult to see examples of both active and passive avoidance behaviors at home and at school. A child who has been consistently punished for playing with the controls of the television set soon learns to leave them alone (passive avoidance). Punishment for copying the work of another student can cause passive avoidance of that behavior, also. Active avoidance behavior is shown in instances when a child eats his meal or studies his schoolwork to avoid punishment. With children, however, problems arise in the use of punishment to control behavior. Children at home and at school have more alternative behavior choices than do rats in a cage. The child who is blocked from the television set may soon find equally unproductive ways to spend his time. Students punished for cheating still have several other ways of trying to pass without learning the material of the test. Food eaten under duress has a way of coming up and making a mess to be cleaned by the punishing mother. And the student who is coerced into studying seldom makes much headway. Thus, fear as a means of controlling human behavior, while it remains in constant use, has unpredictable results. Occasionally, punishment seems to be effective in shaping behavior, but the results are not always predictable.

For information relating to the effects of fear in school learning, we must turn to studies of punishment as a reinforcer. Studies of this type seldom employ the concept of fear in their discussion, but fear nonetheless is involved in producing the outcomes. It is not possible to find studies with human subjects paralleling the animal studies from which the empirical data concerning fear have been collected. When shock, or any other form of physical punishment has been applied to human subjects, it has generally been of lower intensity than the punishments to which animals have been subjected. Nevertheless, in studies showing the effect of punishment, there have been important findings.

In a series of experiments designed to examine the influence of electric shock on visual perception, McNamara, Solley, and Long (1958) found that perception was negatively influenced by the intensity of the shock. When the shock reached a certain potency, there was a rapid decline in the subjects' perceptions of the visual stimulus before them at the time. Mangan (1959), using visual stimuli and electric shock in much the same manner, found that mild shock tended to improve, or at least to maintain perception, whereas intense shock destroyed it. These findings are in general agreement with the findings from studies of reward and punishment. Summarizing the literature concerning these effects, Marshall (1965) points out that under mild negative reinforcement, performance sometimes improves.

When one tries to read the literature concerning reward and punishment, a problem is encountered. Large numbers of studies report no significant difference in the effect of the two types of treatment on learning. Solution to the problem seems to be in the intensity of the punishment used. When the finding is that punishment tends to improve performance, then one must conclude that the punishment used with the particular subjects of the study did not prove to be sufficiently strong to inhibit learning. This does not mean that the same punishment used with a different group of students would prove to be equally mild and have the same effect. Based upon the research information available to us at this time, it is safe to conclude that when the punishment is mild enough to serve only as a cue to wrong responses, then its effect will be positive and will facilitate learning. However, when it is strong enough to create significant fear, the effect is to destroy perception which is at the heart of much of the learning involved in schoolwork.

It is not a simple matter to assess the intensity of anxiety. One of the first attempts to measure and study it is found in the work of Janet Taylor (1953) who developed the Manifest Anxiety Scale. By her definition (Taylor 1956), anxiety is a drive with increments which are directly related to levels of performance. Stating in simpler terms, Taylor theorized that when subjects use a correct approach to solving problems, those with high drive (high anxiety) excel over those with low drive (low anxiety). Her theory has an underlying assumption that each individual has a level of anxiety which is relatively constant and disposed to exercise a positive motivational influence upon any task the individual is given to perform. Her position has been supported by Spence and Farber (1953) and by Spence and Taylor (1953). These studies report that high scores on the Manifest Anxiety Scale were associated with high performance and low scores with low performance. It must be pointed out, however, that the tasks employed were not characterized by complex intellectual processes but, rather, by rote memory and conditioning.

There is not agreement as to the nature of anxiety or its effects. Other authors contend that anxiety is more specific than Taylor describes it to be, and they disagree that it is always facilitating. In the belief that Taylor was wrong in her basic assumptions about the measurement of anxiety, Mandler and Sarason (1952) developed a different approach to measurement. On the assumption that anxiety functions relative to the specific tasks given a subject to perform, they developed a test of anxiety about the taking of a test (Test Anxiety Scale). Their scale results in a score derived from the responses of subjects who are asked to recall the intensity of certain feelings and experiences they have had in taking various kinds of tests. When the Taylor Manifest Anxiety Scale and the Mandler and Sarason Test Anxiety Scale have been compared, the latter has shown the best prediction of performance on tests (Mandler and Sarason 1952; Alpert and Haber 1960). These findings have been used to conclude that anxiety is not as generalized as Taylor believed.

Still another viewpoint concedes that anxiety may prove to facilitate performance but maintains that there are debilitating effects of anxiety, also. Alpert and Haber (1960) present a test which has two subsets of items: one subtest measures facilitating anxiety, and the other is directed at debilitating anxiety. They validate the facilitating anxiety subtest by showing that high scores predict test and grade-point averages. Debilitating anxiety scores have a negative relationship with performance. In a study of the effects of failure on the expectation of success, Feather (1963) found that facilitating anxiety correlated with the prediction of success despite increasing failure experience. Persons with high scores on the facilitating subtest of the anxiety test tended to predict that they would succeed on subsequent trials even though their failures were mounting consistently. Feather also noted that the expectation of failure and the fear of failure tended to develop for all subjects with increased failure experience.

Other studies have reported characteristics of anxious subjects in learning situations, characteristics which are important for teachers to note. In one of the better studies on the subject, Grimes and Allinsmith (1961) found that highly anxious children work best in highly structured conditions. Testing this finding with another population, Kight and Sassenrath (1966) used programmed instruction as the structured situation. They found that students with high motivation for achievement or with high test anxiety required less time on a program, made fewer errors, and received higher scores on the postmeasure of short-term retention. In his review of several studies of the effects of anxiety, Sarason (1960) noted that as task complexity increases, the highly anxious student tends to perform at progressively lower levels.

Normal children and adults actually seek mild frustrations and anxiety and get pleasure from the experience. A feeling of frustration and tension is raised during the activity of solving puzzles and problems, and yet people return to them time and again. Games of chance are popular money-makers in carnivals because of the mild anxiety they provoke. Most of those who linger around the games and continue to try to win are aware that the prizes given for winning are of small cash value. Why does a driver risk passing in heavy traffic when he is in no real hurry to reach his destination or when, in fact, he may have no particular destination? Even though there is some social value in being seen as a winner, there remains a lot of risk-taking and self-imposed frustration to explain. The relationship between fear and curiosity has been pointed out by Whiting and Mowrer (1943) and by Berlyne (1950). Maximum curiosity is aroused by circumstances which contain a degree of uncertainty. At the same time, too much uncertainty and risk tend to prevent exploration and involvement. In his study of the motivational determinants of risk-taking, Atkinson (1968) found that tasks or behaviors with little uncertainty have low motivational value as do tasks wherein the uncertainty is very high, but that tasks with a moderate degree of risk tend to have the strongest attraction. There is no question but that risk and frustration produce excitement and that excitement has a positive effect in motivation if the excitement in not too intense.

Curiosity and Exploration

Everywhere there is evidence that a large proportion of time, energy, and money is spent in activities involving curiosity, exploration, and play. Entertainment and leisure time enterprises capitalize upon the avid interest shown by large numbers of people in pursuit of real or imaginary adventure, manipulation of gadgets, and exploration of caves, fun houses, reconstructed villages, and mountain trails. Visiting new countries and territories, and even exploring outer space have been motivated in part by man's need to see what lies beyond his immediate horizons. As positive proof of the thrill involved in exploration, one has only to watch while astronauts cavort about on the surface of the moon examining rocks and testing their own bodily reactions in a strange gravitational field. Even the television viewer gets a vicarious thrill from viewing the experience. Existence of curiosity as a strong motive was recognized early in the study of motivation and was listed as a secondary drive by Tolman (1932) but, until 1950, it was scarcely mentioned as a topic for investigation. Since that time, it has gained a significant place in the concern of researchers and writers interested in motivation.

Why did psychology turn its attention to curiosity and exploration as topics for study? In his intensive work on the subject, Fowler (1965) noted that a goodly portion of man's behavior is typified, not by those activities that sustain life but "... rather by those pronounced and prominent tendencies that it had to explore, to investigate, or in general, to seek out new forms of stimulation" (p. 3). The long delay in studying these important aspects of man's behavior has slowed the understanding of human psychology, but this is less important than the condition which now seems to pervade research on curiosity. Instead of investigating these newly rediscovered needs in human beings, too much time and energy is devoted to the study of animal curiosity and exploration. It is difficult to find well-organized studies of the nature and effect of curiosity in human beings, despite the clear evidence that it can be investigated.

What are the conditions, internal and external, that lead to exploratory behavior? Various theories have been advanced, but only a few have been supported with data from human subjects. Exploration and investigation go on, according to Berlyne (1960), as a way of selecting the stimuli to which one responds at a given time and place. Primary importance is placed upon the kind and intensity of stimulus material in the surroundings and its effect in activating and directing behavior. Novel stimuli affect the organism to arouse the drive condition known as curiosity. After continued exposure to the novel stimulus, curiosity diminishes or loses its drive quality. Knowledge that appears to support Berlyne's viewpoint is found in studies which demonstrate that human subjects will perform tasks to get to look at pictures as a reward (Lindsley 1956). More evidence has been accumulated from research with rats (Robinson 1957, 1959, 1961) and with monkeys (Butler 1957). It is the opinion of Fowler (1965) that the purpose of exploration lies in the simple need to alter whatever stimulus pattern has been impinging on the organism. This belief, by implication, is based upon a concept of boredom which is, in effect, a condition of saturation of the senses with whatever has been in the experience pattern for some time. Evidence to support the need for altering the stimulus pattern has been found in the very popular study reported by Bexton, Heron, and Scott (1954). Human subjects were paid to "do nothing" for an extended period of time while their basic needs were cared for and they were kept comfortable. Only a few subjects could remain under these conditions for more than two to three days. An intense desire for stimulation of even a very simple kind was evident.

Still another possible explanation of exploratory behavior is in the earlier discussion of anxiety. There it was mentioned that a component of fear has been noted in exploratory behavior. Curiosity may be a motivator because a token amount of controllable anxiety is raised in anticipation of the unknown and in the pursuit of exploration. Then there is the theory of White (1959) who proposes two reasons man would alter his stimulus pattern:

(1) to satisfy an inherent need to interact with the environment, and
(2) to increase his effectiveness and competence in dealing with the environment.

Actually, the varieties of exploratory behavior are numerous, and no single theory can include the subtleties of them all.

Exploratory behaviors have been set apart into certain types and classified with appropriate terms. Four of the classifications made by Berlyne (1960) appear to have significance for teachers: specific, diversive, inspective, and inquisitive. When the behavior is in pursuit of some known or expected goal, such as a particular piece to fit into a puzzle or the solution to an arithmetic problem, Berlyne calls it *specific exploration*. Just "fooling around," aimless wandering, rummaging, and other forms of exploration where the behavior itself provides the only incentive are referred to as *diversive exploration*. *Inspective exploration* is a term used to refer to behavior such as "looking at," "listening to," "feeling of," and other nonspecific sensory surveys of environmental materials. The more specific behaviors described by the terms "looking for," "listening for," and "feeling for" are referred to as *inquisitive behaviors*.

Specific exploration, while it may be the type most frequently used by human beings, has been a neglected area of study. We know by observation that when an individual sets out to find a specific part for a machine or a puzzle, his behavior may take the form of trial and error, or structuring and insight. Our concern here, however, is the motivational value and not the particular solution behavior observed to occur in exploration. In the case of *specific exploration,* the motivational value or strength comes more from the completed object or goal itself than from the act of exploring. In fact, there may be very little persever-ance when the seeker knows what he seeks but meets frustration in his efforts to find it. Unless the goal object holds high value itself, the exploration is likely to stop or be diverted into some more pleasurable activity.

Most of the study of human behavior has involved intrinsic or *diversive exploration*. Many writers have referred to the early work of Piaget as a forerunner in the study of infantile investigatory behavior. He used the term *secondary circular reactions* to refer to the infant's tendency to repeat actions which bring about interesting results. At a subsequent level of development, the child begins to vary his behavior deliberately to observe the outcome (*tertiary circular reaction*). Often, it is evident that the child knows what effect to look for and that he has a set of expectancies which have been developed as a hypothesis to be tested by the new action. These experiences are excellent examples of intrinsic motivation and serve very well to illustrate what White (1959) meant when he wrote of "dealing effectively with the environment."

Inspective behavior is a survey technique ordinarily employed when the organism is simply taking in information. It is an induction process used when no specific characterisitc has as yet been identified for more detailed exploration. Inspective behaviors have the function of building up a reservoir of data for further consideration. Knowledge relating to distinctive characteristics such as size, shape, color, texture, weight, and specific detail are then used to build discriminatory learn-ings (the ability to pick one object or idea from among several).

Inquisitive behavior seems to emerge from a preconceived idea about the relationship between two or more objects or concepts. Before inquiry can be made, one must have sufficient knowledge to be able to formulate answerable questions or to design actions that will lead to observable changes in the environment.

Research into the matter of curiosity of children has been limited to a few studies of the nature of stimuli which seem to arouse the drive condition. In a study of sixty nursery school children, Mendel (1965) found that children in the age range of three to five years selected toys of high novelty over those with which they were more familiar. Smock and Holt (1962) showed pictures with varying degrees of ambiguity and incongruity to forty-four first grade children. The children could con-trol the conditions to the extent of signaling for a change from a present picture, and they could call for the repeat of a previous picture. It was found that pictures with high novelty elicited more "repeat" signals than did the pictures with low novelty. In a study by Maw and Maw (1962), it was demonstrated that fifth grade children rated by teachers, peers, and themselves as being high in curiosity preferred unbalanced and unusual designs over those with fewer unusual qualities. These findings substantiate the ideas of Berlyne (1960) presented in the discussion of the arousal effects of visual stimuli.

Discrepancy Theories

There are three contemporary theories of motivation which are built on some form of cognitive discrepancy. There is in psychology a continuing tendency to see a need in human beings to maintain an organization or equilibrium in psychological life as well as in the biological systems. Since Cannon first proposed the concept of *homeostasis* in his famous work, *The Wisdom of the Body*, in 1932, others have sought to apply the concept to man's psychological behavior as well as to his need for food, water, and other life-sustaining necessities. One of the first major attempts to build a theory of motivation with this concept central to it was presented by Snygg and Combs (1949). We have discussed their theory under the concept of basic need. At this point, however, its relationship to other theories based upon the avoidance of discord should become evident. In individual psychology, the motive of man's behavior is seen as the prevention of conflict, disorganization, inconsistency, dissonance, discrepancy, and other forms of mismatch between things as they are observed to be and as the individual wants them to be. To do more justice to this theory, we must point out that those who espouse it tend to phrase it in positive terms. They see people behaving in ways designed to maintain and enhance themselves and not as avoiders of threats to their balance and security.

The concept of competence, as it is presented by White (1959), is built on a similar thought. He describes competence as the fitness or ability to deal effectively with the environment. Then he refers to a statement by Angyal (1941) that man's basic motive is to assimilate the environment, to transform his surroundings, and to gain control of it as a means of self-improvement. While these statements do not imply a condition of homeostasis, they do infer a degree of discrepancy between the individual's desires for himself and his perceptions of the environment. This disparity is seen as the source of energy and arousal whereby the individual effects changes in himself and his surroundings. When this idea is applied to the desire to master certain areas of knowledge, to formulate and solve problems, we arrive at Ausubel's (1968) definition of the term *cognitive drive*. Ausubel considers that cognitive drives or interests are acquired through particular experiences, and he sees their relationship with learning as reciprocal. They are learned because they have resulted in rewards and, in turn, they motivate further learning.

Still another viewpoint based upon discord is Festinger's (1957, 1968) concept of *cognitive dissonance*. In this theory, human motivation is explained in terms of the difference between one's behavior and his own evaluation of that behavior. Ordinarily, there is discord or dissonance between the two cognitions. This discrepancy constitutes a source of energy which the individual may call upon to produce actions to (1) modify his behavior, or (2) modify his evaluation of that behavior. In the words of Festinger (1968), ". . . this dissonance can be reduced if the organism can persuade himself that he really likes the behavior in which he engaged or if he enhances for himself the value of what he has obtained as a result of his actions. There is, of course, another way to reduce the dissonance, namely, for the organism to change his behavior" (p. 383). This viewpoint amounts to an admission that, since motivation derives from the difference between what one sees in his own behavior and what he values highest, there is a degree of dissatisfaction with oneself necessary before change or action will occur. Martire (1956) found that students with the strongest achievement motivation also had the largest discrepancy between their real and their ideal self-image and between their actual and their desired traits of achievement behavior. While this position may be defensible in terms of a potential behavioral change or for action to modify the environment, it fails in practicality. Dissonance, if it is of low order, is not likely to bring about action because the extent of arousal is insufficient to activate the organism. On the other hand, great dissonance is likely to produce low arousal, also. The curve of relationship between dissonance and change of behavior or values seems to be of the same general nature as that of the arousal-learning curve, an inverted U. Highest effective motivation lies in moderate amounts of dissonance. There must be enough discrepancy to make action seem worthwhile, but at the same time, there must be a perceived possibility that action will bring about the desired result. When the dissonance is too great, the organism may well decide that any effort to change it is useless. Or, it is possible that in instances of high discrepancy between what is desired and what is evident, the organism is caught in an anxiety state which turns its energies away from constructive change and turns them toward defensive behaviors.

Reinforcement

It is common knowledge that certain events following particular behaviors increase the chances that the behavior will occur again. In recent years, teachers have come to recognize the term *reinforcement* as referring to this phenomenon.[1] What teachers may not be aware of is the varied and complex role reinforcement plays in student motiva-

---

1. In Chapter 1, there is a discussion of basic terminology which need not be repeated here.

tion. In fact, some treatments of motivation speak of "motivation and reward" as though motivation and reinforcement stand apart as distinctly different concepts. In truth, there are real differences between the terms, but to ignore the relationship between need and reward is to miss an important aspect of motivation. There exists such a large body of writing relating to the many facets of reinforcement that only a token amount of it can be reviewed here. After a few basic points have been made, only the major thoughts concerning reinforcement as it relates to student motivation can be treated.

It is common to begin by distinguishing between primary and secondary reinforcers. A *primary reinforcer* is an object or event that directly satisfies (wholly or partially) a need of the individual. There are many more events or objects that have reinforcement value, not in themselves, but because they have become associated in some way with primary reinforcers. These symbols or signals are called *secondary reinforcers*. There may be very little value in trying to make clear distinction between the two.

Before we could identify a primary reinforcer, we would have to decide what the primary needs are, a task which has become difficult, if not impossible. Furthermore, a secondary reinforcer can acquire a primary quality by becoming important in and of itself. A frequent example is the tendency to acquire money or other symbols of social or economic success, not for their symbolic value but simply as a possession. There are many kinds of events and objects which may function as reinforcers for student behavior. They vary, from real objects through the entire range of auditory, visual, and concrete symbols of social and emotional significance, to the knowledge that an answer is right, and on to the good feeling and satisfaction over a job well done. What will motivate one student as an incentive may have no motivational value at all for another. Therefore, no discussion of reinforcement can tell a teacher what special reinforcer to use with a particular student. It is possible, however, to show that other aspects of reinforcement can be predicted to have certain noticeable effects in student behavior.

When we read or speak with others about reinforcement, we are likely to see or hear the words *tangible, intangible, extrinsic,* and *intrinsic.* All too often, only vague understanding of their meanings is communicated, and it is not altogether uncommon to find the words used carelessly. Ordinarily, the distinction between tangible and intangible reinforcers simply refers to the quality either of having or of not having substance (made of organic or inorganic matter). Objects, a touch, a paper star, a coin, or token are all examples of tangible reinforcers. On the other hand, a word, a smile, a nod, or a wink might be classed as intangible reinforcers. Actually, the distinction is seldom very clear, and research based upon the effectiveness of tangible and intangible reinforcers must be examined carefully before it is generalized.

Quite apart from the substantive quality is the other dichotomy of intrinsic-extrinsic reinforcement. Webster's International Dictionary defines *intrinsic* as "within, internal, belonging to the inmost constitution or essential nature of a thing." The term is quite consistent in its meaning regardless of the field of knowledge in which it is used; therefore, in psychology and education, its meaning ought to maintain the same consistency. Intrinsic reinforcers, then, are cues inherent in the learning process itself, and furthermore, they are essential and not extraneous ingredients imposed from outside the learning process. Intrinsic reinforcers can be tangible or intangible. A student who polishes the metal surface of a gear to be used as an essential part of a machine may rub the surface with his finger, feel its smoothness, or find an irregularity, thus getting *tangible intrinsic reinforcement*. Another student, having developed an expectancy that when he connects two independent operations in mathematics, the solution to his problem will be one step nearer, performs the action and gains insight to the answer, thus obtaining *intangible intrinsic reinforcement*. Webster's Dictionary defines *extrinsic* as "not contained in or belonging to a body, external, outward, unessential." Thus, extrinsic reinforcers are not a part of the internal learning process itself but are imposed from the outside. They can also be either tangible or intangible. A student who solves an arithmetic problem or who correctly spells a word and receives a piece of candy or a star on his chart gets a *tangible extrinsic reinforcer*. When a smile or a confirming reaction is given by the teacher, it is an example of an intangible extrinsic reinforcer.

Unfortunately, the writing and research on these topics have seldom involved a careful distinction and, as a result, the findings fail to tell us as much as we would like to know. In many cases, what are really intangible extrinsic reinforcers are called intrinsic, and it is concluded that certain doubtful effects actually occur. The extent of our knowledge is limited to a few pieces of research evidence. One of the most consistent findings is that there is a social class difference in response to reinforcement. Children from lower-class homes have been found to respond most favorably to extrinsic material reinforcers, whereas students from the middle class respond more favorably to intangible reinforcers (Douvan 1956; Hoffman, Mitsos, and Pratz 1958; Green and Stachnik 1968).

4

The Achievement Motive

Discovery that the achievement motive could be induced and measured was reported by David C. McClelland and others (1949). Their work initiated research of real significance for education, although it has not been recognized by educational psychologists until recently. Since 1950, several aspects of the achievement motive have been explored. Conditions of infancy and early childhood have been studied for their contribution to the development of motivation to achieve. High and low levels of motivation have been examined as they relate to other variables of behavior. Studies continue to contribute useful knowledge about a wide range of achievement-related conditions. Many of the most significant findings are reported here because they appear to be outgrowths of the most relevant approach to the investigation of school achievement.

While achievement motivation is not limited specifically to the behaviors of schoolwork, the relationship is close. N-ach has been defined by Heckhausen (1967) as " . . . the striving to increase, or to keep as high as possible, one's own capability in all activities in which a standard of excellence is thought to apply and when the execution of such activities can, therefore, either succeed or fail" (p. 4). School achievement, although it is only one aspect of the larger achievement domain, certainly occupies a significant place in the active life of most individuals. Academic learning in school is an activity to which a standard of excellence has traditionally been applied, and success and failure have been strongly associated with school. Therefore, schoolwork fits very well with the criteria Heckhausen uses in his definition. In this chapter, information found in studies of achievement motivation is examined in terms of its meaning and application in education. School people should be able to apply much of the theory and many of the research findings to improve their understanding of academic motivation.

Assessment of Achievement Motivation

The study of n-ach had its real beginning with McClelland's demonstration in 1949 that an experimentally induced "need for mastery" could be measured with a projective test. Achievement strivings had been one aspect of a larger interpretation made from Thematic Apperception Tests since Murray (1943) developed the test. But McClelland (1949) and his associates selected four pictures and used them with male college students specifically to study their achievement needs. Since that time, other projective tests and several objective question-answer types have been used in research with subjects ranging in age from preschool to adulthood. The research findings presented later in this chapter come from studies using both kinds of instruments, but the projective tests have contributed most of the data. It is not possible in the space available to present samples of tests and their interpretations. And yet, it seems necessary to have a brief explanation of the projective technique if the reader is to understand and appreciate the findings that follow. For a more complete description and case material, the reader should consult McClelland et al. (1953). A listing of several objective tests of motivation may be found in the test and research findings presented by Russell (1969).

Commonly, a subject is shown a picture on a screen or on a card. Directions ask him to tell or write a story (original) relating to the content of the picture. In the imaginative stories, there may be content which can be examined for its display of achievement strivings. First, the scorer must decide which elements of the stories have references and information sufficient to justify scoring. These elements must be clear indication that a story character is striving "in competition with some standard of excellence." Four qualities may be found in episodes useful in assessment:

1. Winning, or at least meeting, the competition of others must be actually stated or implied as a primary concern of a character in the story.

2. A self-imposed standard of excellence against which the subject strives is a scorable quality.

3. A story character may be attempting to accomplish an unusual task, such as an invention or a creative work of some kind.

4. Striving to attain a long-range goal qualifies the episode for scoring, also.

Episodes qualifying as scorable are examined for their contribution in each of the following ways:

1. Are the striving activities successful, unsuccessful, or of doubtful outcome?

2. Did the story character anticipate success or failure at the outset of his activity?

3. If the goal-seeking activity was thwarted, what was the source of the frustrating agent?

4. Did the story character receive significant aid from anyone in attaining his goal? If so, what was the source and nature of the aid?

5. What emotions or feelings were expressly associated with the success, failure, or undetermined outcome?

6. Did the achievement theme occupy a central or peripheral position in the story?

Information thus accumulated is used to assess the achievement motive in its several dimensions. Level or intensity of the need to achieve is estimated in terms of the frequency and intensity of striving present in the imagery of the stories. The degree of optimism as to the outcome of achievement efforts is estimated from the outlook of those characters who show the striving behavior and from the outcome of their actions. Both intensity and anticipation are important qualities to know about the achievement motive of individuals.

Development of Achievement Motivation

Conditions which qualify to be classed as motivations are relatively stable qualities of the personality, once they reach development. Here we are concerned about the deeper underlying condition rather than about the momentary variation of achievement striving. Essentially, the motivational quality seeming to be relatively constant is that which characterizes the wide range of achievement behavior rather than the immediate situational arousal shown at a particular time. How does the achievement motive develop? What are the conditions from which it springs? There is general agreement that it is learned from very early experience and that it is modified by later learnings. The vagueness and overall responsiveness of this motive suggests a large affective component in its make up. Therefore, it must have its origins in a period when the child experiences mass action and generalized feeling, that is, in infancy. As adults, we are unable to recall, with any clarity, the feelings of that period, and thus our understanding of it must be based upon inferences from other sources.

From psychoanalytic techniques, Freud gathered a rich body of evidence concerning infantile pleasure strivings connected with basic body functions. It is to him we often turn for descriptions of the way in which the infant's first awareness of himself and of his body security and well-being grow out of the experiences of pleasure and pain. The generally accepted viewpoint of Freud and his followers, according to Ribble (1944), is that "these pleasure strivings exist from the beginning of extrauterine life." Muller (1969), describing the infant as Freud discovered him to be, says, "This child was not a miniature adult but a totally different being. Nor was he innocent, but a creature obstinately bent on his own satisfaction, a kind of powerful, cruel force, ready to smash everything in his pursuit of gratification, enslaving others or becoming their slave, according to his particular inclinations, outside time, outside reality, more a thing than a person, and bound at some deep level to the life force itself" (p. 70).

Learning acquired during infancy is the outgrowth of pleasure-pain associations, with only vague awareness of the conditions that produce them. Later, as language and the ability to use simple symbolic processes develop, the child is more acutely aware of the differences between feelings and situations. Thus, learning at the early stage of development has strong and permeating influences which are resistant to change. Lacking specificity, these learning experiences tend only to establish a mood or expectancy in the child. Wendt (1961) discovered a relationship between "risk-taking" behavior in individuals and the predictability of a mother's behavior in this prelanguage era of the child's life.

From Wendt's findings, we can assume that there is, in the development of the achievement motive, an imprinting of the anticipation that things will work out predictably for the child. Mothers who are consistent in their reactions to infant demands for gratification provide the child a base line from which he can learn to expect relief with a given amount of delay. It is from this circumstance that the child gets his first perspective of the passage of time. If gratification and release from feelings of discomfort or pain come after a reasonable period, other things being favorable, the infant builds an expectancy that delay will produce a desirable outcome. The period of delay of reward can be extended gradually without losing the child's positive expectancy. If, to the contrary, there is no regularity to the gratification pattern, then no expectancy for success can be developed by the child because there is no relative constancy of the duration of the delay. Anxiety is created in the child, and he cannot perceive that what he does (tolerate discomfort) has any influence on what happens to him. Thus, robbed of the opportunity to learn that the struggle going on within him to postpone gratification can end within relatively fixed periods of delay, he has no base from which to develop optimism and a positive expectance.

Development through Expectancy

The relationship between expectancy and achievement behavior has been well established. Expectancy is a result of previous reinforcements of certain behaviors. In addition, it is a motivator of subsequent actions. Crandall, Good, and Crandall (1964) have shown that adult reactions and nonreactions to children's achievement behaviors have a strong influence upon the later expectations children have for their achievement efforts. Feather (1966) is only one of many researchers who have demonstrated that positive reinforcement or success increases the expectancy of the same condition in future actions. Failure or punishment decreases the expectation of success. The dual role of expectancy as both an effect of previous reward and the motivator for future actions has been thoroughly investigated by Crandall and McGhee (1968). Reporting the results of five separate studies, they concluded that there is "a gradient of expectancy generalization" which, in their case, may have caused the increasing predictive power when the criterion measures of reinforcement and achievement became more alike. In their research, as in many other studies, grades given by teachers were used in one instance as a reinforcement, and in another instance, as the measure of achievement. They, like Battle (1966), and Todd, Terrell, and Frank (1962), found that students' expectancies for certain marks were strongly related to the marks they actually received. Battle reports relationships ranging from .74 to .85 between students' expected marks in mathematics and English and the grades they received in those subjects.

Development through Parental Demands
Parental demands and tasks begin to be imposed upon the child quite early in his life. These are made in the atmosphere of a total parent-child relationship. They are accompanied by certain amounts of forcefulness and consistency from the parents. It is from the child's success or failure in meeting these encounters and from the rewards or punishments he receives that his first achievement motives take further form. In the face of strong demands, he can persist in his efforts to get his own way and fail, thus, in all likelihood, diminishing the amount of reward in terms of loving affection he might have received. Or, on the other hand, he can come, rather readily, to accept the limitations imposed upon him and strive to meet them favorably. This is more likely to result in emotional rewards for him. The success he has in performing the tasks set for him by his parents, and the rewards bestowed upon him, influence his future task behaviors. In their discussion of these matters, and in summary of the results from the study of 500 children, Argyle and Robinson (1962) say "emotional rewards for achievement and punishment for nonachievement in a rigid nonindulgent setting, and experience of success at tasks may all contribute to n-ach" (p. 120).

An earlier study of boys nine to eleven years of age and the nature of their parents' behaviors was reported by Rosen and D'Andrade (1959). They found that parents of boys with high achievement motivation were more interested and concerned with their sons' performances, showed more affection, set up standards of excellence, expected more, and reinforced more with praise and punishment than was the case with parents of boys with low motivation for achievement. There was a tendency among parents of highly motivated sons to give more hints and encouragement. Similar findings are reported from the research of Heilbrun and Waters (1968) which support the view that both nurturance and standards of performance are important elements for the development of an achievement motive.

Other conditions relating to the development of n-ach have also been studied. Winterbottom (1958), studying boys, found that, while mothers of high n-ach sons did not impose more demands, they did require performance of them at an earlier age. Thus, in effect, they made stronger demands at a given point in development. Also, by moving task accomplishment to an earlier age, they moved it to a period of stronger affective content, and this may have contributed more to generalization of the task behavior than it would have if accomplishment had been left until later.

A comment frequently made by parents is that their demands and expectancies were stronger and harsher on their firstborn than on those children who came later. However, Munz and his associates (1968) found no relationship between ordinal position in the family and achievement motivation. In a detailed study of early and late maturing boys, Mussen and Jones (1958) found no significant difference in the achievement motive between the two groups. Girls are generally found to exceed boys in their level of achievement motivation, and there is a large body of information showing that mothers place earlier demands upon girls to master the independence training tasks—to walk sooner, and, in general, to become independent with more success at an earlier age.

Effects of Success and Failure

Success and failure as they affect persistence and goal-setting behavior have been studied with relatively consistent findings. Nursery school children show more persistence at tasks after success and praise for performances of successively more difficult tasks (Kiester 1938). Sears (1940) reported similar findings in terms of raised levels of aspiration following success in previous tasks. Failure to achieve brings about a decrease in level of aspiration, as shown by Ausubel and Schiff (1955). It is well accepted that these conditions hold true in early age. Findings indicate that the child remains sensitive to his early successes and failures and sets his goals accordingly far into life. In their description of longitudinal studies, Kagan and Moss (1962) note a striving for success and a fear of failure from the age of six years upward. In a study of success and failure, Rosenzweig (1933) found a tendency to overcome failure in children from four to fourteen years of age. Weiner (1965) found that subjects of high n-ach persisted longer and worked faster following failure, and that those of low motivation worked better following continued success.

Setting Standards of Performance

Another aspect of the development of achievement motivation is the process whereby children come to set their own "standards of excellence." That children are influenced in standard-setting by the models they observe has been confirmed by Bandura and Kupers (1964). In the study by Rosen and D'Andrade already cited, the parents (models) of highly motivated children were more competitive, more involved, and took more pleasure in problem-solving tasks. In short, they were striving, competent persons. Similar findings have been reported by Argyle and Robinson (1962).

Also, we can observe from the work of Liebert and Allen (1967) that children acquire standards from direct rewards. Children who experience a reward system that is sufficiently consistent begin to create an internalized expectancy which amounts to a standard. If successively higher expectancies are developed, then high internalized standards of performance are established in the child. Working with a group of eighty-four boys, seven to eleven years of age, Bee and Calle (1968) sought to determine the relative effectiveness of modeling and direct reward procedures. They found that both methods were effective. Their direct reward group exhibited more standard-setting behavior, which may have been the result of differences in the social backgrounds of the subjects. Their subjects were primarily from the lower strata of socioeconomic conditions. Other research cited in a later discussion concerned with motivation and disadvantaged students speaks more directly about this matter. Let it be sufficient at this point to say that children from lower-class homes tend to respond more favorably to extrinsic rewards. This is a likely explanation of the finding by Bee and Calle. It does not seem to be a critical matter which method is more effective if each works sufficiently well. The main concern here is that, for achievement motivation to be evidenced in the behavior of an individual, that individual must have a tendency to set a standard of performance for himself. And it is apparent that children learn to set these standards when they receive rewards for successes. Also, if they observe that a model sets a standard of performance and rewards himself for reaching it, they will copy this behavior themselves.

A matter not as yet established is the extent to which children can acquire standard-setting behavior after they reach school age. We have cause to believe that since very early affective experience establishes the atmosphere for expectancy, the achievement motive is quite firmly set at that time. Does this mean that teachers can have no influence upon it? It might be quite difficult, if not impossible, under the usual school program to bring about a complete reversal of earlier behaviors. However, since most research subjects who show modified behavior are in the age range from six years upward, there is evidence that strong influences upon the achievement motive remain possible, and even likely, if deliberate procedures are applied to produce them. But, are situational improvements generalized to become a part of a child's total personality and an influence upon his subsequent achievement behaviors in new situations? This has yet to be answered in specific terms, but a good case could be constructed to support a positive outlook. However, to have its maximum impact upon the child, the school must do its work on the parents as well as upon the child. Effects of early childhood experiences upon later behavior make it ever more imperative that schools or some other agency reach into homes and become an influence for the benefit of children who are there.

Success- or Failure-Oriented Motivation

Hope for success and fear of failure, each is a condition that can account for achievement behavior. From the viewpoint of mental health, we prefer to see students hope for success and to expect that their actions will produce favorable results. Instead, many never experience this positive aspect of motivation. The haunting fear that failure awaits them organizes their behavior around attempts to avoid it. Superficially, these two orientations may seem to be similar. Both can lead to high motivation and significant achievement. In simple task situations, the behavior may be very much the same regardless of which of the two orientations spawns it. And yet we realize there are differences. In what ways do the success-oriented behaviors stand apart from the failure-oriented behaviors? Do both types approach tasks in the same way? How do individuals become either success or failure oriented? Should teaching behavior be modified to suit the one or the other? These are questions that the teacher must consider.

Research to provide at least tentative answers to these questions has been meager indeed. Perhaps those who conduct studies in motivation have not as yet seen the special significance these problems hold for education and for the welfare of children. A projective assessment of the achievement motive makes it possible to distinguish the success-oriented individual from the one who is striving to avoid failure. This possibility has resulted in a limited number of studies, most of which are reported in Heckhausen (1967). Many of the findings are the results of studies conducted in Germany, and the original reports are not available in translation. In the discussion that follows, the findings come from Heckhausen, except in cases that are cited from other sources. Space is not available to present the detailed account of each research study, but those findings which appear to be significant for teachers are discussed.

Goal Setting

Success-oriented individuals, given the opportunity to set their own goals, make their selections on the probability of achieving success. They tend to evaluate the difficulty of attaining a goal on the basis of their own past performance and to take into consideration the immediate conditions which might influence the outcome. Tasks in the range of moderate difficulty are most attractive and produce the most stimulation for them. As these individuals mature, they set increasingly more distant goals. Tasks requiring planning and decision-making are preferred over short-term and simple tasks. These are qualities which become characteristics as the individual develops, and they may not be expected to describe the young child who has had few goal choices to make. Just how the success-oriented personality develops has not been well established. One popular assumption is that very young children whose independence training has been characterized by continued success develop an optimistic and wholesome attitude toward goals and task behaviors. Increasingly more frequent occasions for the child to select his goals and activities is thought to lead to more realistic goal-setting behaviors. How early the pattern is established has not been determined. Heckhausen (1967) says

> ... it seems that even small children show a disposition to prefer either a more goal-oriented or defense-oriented method of resolving conflicts—a preference which results in a strengthening of success—approaching or failure—avoiding motivational tendencies.

Failure-oriented individuals set their goals on the likelihood of avoiding failure in the situation. Immediate goals requiring very little planning and few decisions are most attractive. The probability of failure is lowest in tasks with these characteristics. Sears (1940), in her study of ten- and twelve-year-olds, found that unsuccessful children with high motivation set either low or very high goals for themselves following failure. That failure-oriented persons choose easier goals following failures requires no explanation since it is a direct and logical outcome. But why do certain of them choose very difficult goals? Perhaps the simplest of several possible explanations is that they anticipate failure again. To fail on a difficult task has more face-saving potential than to fail on an easy task. If one chooses to seek at deeper levels for an explanation, there is the possibility that those who set very high goals for themselves are showing evidence of the disorganizing effects of anxiety. The findings of Martire (1956) and Steiner (1957) support the viewpoint that the difference in the ideal self-image and the actual perceived characteristics in these persons are widely divergent. The goals they set for themselves may be more consistent with their ideal self-image than with the reality of the situation. Hope and the wish that these unrealistically high goals will be attained and will thus support their ideal image may, in this case, be the driving force. Fear as a force in motivation is an exceedingly important topic that has received very little attention, and it comes up for further discussion later.

In terms of the school, what are the implications of differences in goal-setting behavior? The school has a complex role to play in the matter of self-selection of goals. It is well recognized that development toward maturity includes as one critical element a growth toward self-selected, attainable goals. Mental health has as one of its qualities freedom from anxiety. Both of these desirable conditions place the responsibility squarely upon teachers to guide students into goal-setting experiences which foster growth toward realistic attainments and which change fear of failure to anticipation of the pleasure that accompanies success. To accomplish these ends, teachers must become aware of the particular position each student takes in this matter. While it is not possible or likely that a projective test can be given to each child, the teacher can make judgments on his own. Activities involving each student's selection of goals can be utilized in day-to-day observation. Such information should help the teacher to know the students who fit each category. Carefully selected and individually guided experiences can then be directed at the development of a positive outlook and success-directed goal selection.

Approach to Work

There is still another important aspect of the behavior of persons as it relates to their success or failure orientation. After goals have been established, there follows the work of achievement. It is common to see students change behavior once a task is begun. Actions may speed up or slow down. Some students continue in the face of increasing difficulty, whereas others stop or escape from the field by diverting their behavior toward other goals. Task difficulty alone is not sufficient to account for the variations of behavior as they are witnessed. Neither is the level of motivation able to account for all of it. The particular disposition of the individual interacts with the feedback informing him of his progress during task performance. Together, these qualities modify the anticipated outcome and regulate the amount of energy the learner must release into his work to sustain, diminish, or intensify his efforts. Thus, expectancy for success or failure, task difficulty, and feedback information are all important in determining the performance of students.

When influenced to expect success with minimal effort, the failure-oriented person gives up early if success isn't quickly attained. If the task is thought to be difficult, then the failure-oriented student is prone to continue his efforts longer. This finding has particular significance because it goes contrary to the natural tendency of most teachers.

Encouragement which takes the form of creating in the student the anticipation of easy success may be wrong. If the fear of failure is present, perhaps it is better to select easy tasks and play up their difficulty. When success comes readily, the student could then be expected gradually to extend his perseverance for more difficult tasks.

Success-oriented persons are more persistent than are the failure-oriented ones when tasks are difficult. They tend to work quickly and to direct their actions toward task accomplishment, thus conserving time. Failure-oriented individuals tend to waste time, to take less direct action, and yet to feel more confined to the task. They are less able to walk away from the work and relax for a while. Persons who anticipate success may casually leave the task, enjoy a period of play, and then return to complete their work later. These differences in work attitude suggest that the educational approach for success-oriented and failure-oriented students might be most effective for each if specific adaptations were made. Recess periods, frequent interruptions, and the regular period changes of the school day may influence each student differently. Also, setting time limits and speed incentives may encourage the failure-oriented person of high motivation and high potential for achievement to settle for a mediocre performance. In high pressure situations, those persons who tend to be avoiders are less likely to maintain their motivation. Stress conditions raise their anxiety, and this increase added to the anxiety they already feel at the possibility of failure may be too much for them to tolerate. Simply to preserve themselves, they may escape from the pressure by one means or another.

5

Students, Schools, and Motivation

In preceding chapters, we have examined major concepts and theories of human motivation. Now our objective is to bring what we believe to be true about student motives into the school. This task is not an easy one. At the outset, it is necessary to limit our discussion to academic behavior and only incidentally to consider the multitude of other motivations that account for student actions and reactions. Then we must face the fact that, in any group, varieties of motivational forces are at work shaping academic learning. Next we must realize that to understand and deal with motivation requires the patience to look deeply into experiences and to look carefully at the contemporary environment. Observation is the only tool we can employ to get the information we need. Skilled observation and enlightened inferences drawn from what we observe can provide us with more than ordinary insight.

Preschool Conditioners and Early School Life

By the time a child reaches school where we can begin to watch and to influence his reactions, his behavior already suggests a complex psychobiological structure. His basic patterns of reaction to himself and his surroundings are rather firmly established. Nevertheless, if we are to attach meanings to our school observations, we must have an appreciation of the effect that home life has produced in the personality of the child.

Attempting to summarize the influences of the home, or even to contemplate them, is bewildering. Limiting the field to a few admittedly oversimplified areas of concern is the only way we can presume to deal with it here. Perhaps if we confine ourselves to these questions, we will have enough information to make our school observations meaningful:

1. What is the child's status in the home? If he occupies a place of respect, concern, some autonomy, and responsibility, his anticipation of

51

school will likely be positive. If his status is insecure, we can expect him to have difficulty in his school relationships and his motives to direct him away from the main theme of learning.

2. What expectations have the parents held for the child in terms of new learnings? Perhaps they have recognized the child's successes and have helped him to become aware of them, also. This, along with gradually increased expectations in keeping with the child's successes and task difficulties, prepares the child for school learning. Any condition short of these may set the stage for the child to have motivational problems in school.

3. What kind of help has the child received in meeting standards held for him at home? If he has been aided by clues, alternatives, and suggestions, he has had opportunities to develop independence. If things have been done for him, and he has had no choices, it is probable that the result is dependency and difficulty in school.

4. What is the nature of the reward and punishment pattern to which the child has been exposed? If he has grown accustomed to finding some reward in the task itself and to rewarding himself when he satisfies his own expectations, he is well prepared for school learning. On the other hand, if he is in constant need of external rewards or punishments to circumscribe his behavior, school will be confusing.

5. Have his relationships with adults been wholesome and satisfying? If he sees the teacher and others as friendly helpers, he is well prepared to move successfully in his school relationships with them. But if he is too dependent upon or too fearful of adults, his learning behaviors will be adversely affected.

6. Has he learned to enjoy playing and interacting with other children? If so, he will be sufficiently at ease with them to react cooperatively and to learn in the group setting. If not, social interaction is likely to be a problem and a barrier to academic learning.

7. Has his emotional life been reasonably free from extended periods of fear, anger, and rejection? If it has, we can expect enough security and poise for the child to give his attention to academic matters. If life has been quite threatening, the child is most likely to be concerned about his own security and status, leaving little, if any, time and energy for other things.

8. Have his physical needs been cared for? If there have been adequate physical satisfactions, the child should be able to approach social and psychological learning. Hunger and neglect are obvious handicaps in all aspects of the child's life.

9. Have his experiences included a variety of stimuli to which attention has been drawn and meanings attached? Perceptual awareness and curiosity are intensified by exposure and dulled by a lack of it.

10. Has he been helped to understand what he has encountered in his physical and social environment? A desire for knowledge and understanding is increased by verbalization of ideas, questions, explorations, and answers. Confusion and apathy are the probable results of lack of understanding of events that the child encounters.

Adjusting to School

It is immediately evident that children come to school from a variety of backgrounds. Early experiences create in them a diversity of conditions that subsequently influence their lives in school. As adults who have found a home in the school environment, teachers have some difficulty in understanding the plight of children. Why do they not feel as comfortable as we do? At its very best, the school is restrictive enough to create for the child an unreal circumstance, one unlike any other in his life. This strange world is entered with anxiety—a condition typical of any explorer who steps into a new experience. Armed with a set of expectancies drawn from successes and failures of the past and built upon by hearsay, the child makes tentative tests of his surroundings. The behaviors he uses are those previously found to be effective. First, his attention is attracted to the many physical aspects of the area. Then over a period of time, all the movements, sights, sounds, and smells merge into a vague mass. They may be recalled one by one as new meanings are attached to them. Many children encounter the school as an overwhelmingly complex mass of stimuli which must be reacted to with some form of avoidance behavior. To avoid excessive threat, the child may withdraw and show apathy and passivity which last for some length of time. Others quickly select something to which they can react, thereby escaping from the discomfort of the circumstance. Unable to react to each and every stimulus and event in the school day, each child becomes selective. His selections are determined by his own motives and by his perceptions of the environment at the time. A few objects, persons, and events with the most relevance are responded to and recalled. Teachers expect that the significant and meaningful experience will be the one designed to teach the child something that will move him toward the school's objective. However, an inquiry into the highlights of each day would likely prove as disappointing for the teacher as it frequently does for the parent.

Out of the milieu of early school experiences, the child develops a "way of school life" which he is prone to continue for many years. If school turns out to be a place where success is encountered and pleasure is felt, it follows that positive expectancies are created and perpetuated. If, to the contrary, failure, embarrassment, and discomfort are the predominant themes, it is natural that negative expectancies arise. Whatever the child comes to expect, his own perceptions and behaviors tend to fulfill. In the school program or in his relations with teachers, he may find cause to change his expectancies. On the other hand, there is the strong possibility that the child who expects difficulty somehow conveys this feeling to the teacher in nonverbal communication, and that the teacher reacts in ways which make the child's expectations become fact.

By the time children have been in school two or three years, teachers can observe a fairly consistent pattern in their school work. At this early stage, the patterns are relatively simple and consist of at least these five categories:

extrinsic

    (1) works independently to achieve recognized goals;
    (2) works to please the teacher and parents and to meet their expectations;
    (3) works mainly to be affiliated with others and to do what they are doing;
    (4) works under a self-inflicted threat of failure;
    (5) works only when threatened or forced to it.

Later in the school program, other motives come into play, and the patterns become quite complex. We do not as yet have research to describe the motivational conditions of upper grade levels.

The School

To understand the problems of school motivation requires a careful look at the conditions in which teachers and students function. Schools, by their nature, impose limits within which teaching and learning are expected to occur. Physical and academic restrictions grow out of pre-set programs, books, bells, tests, equipment, and classrooms. State laws, administrative policies, and rules laid down by the faculty further limit the atmosphere. If we add to this the personalities of teachers, we have the forces, exclusive of student characteristics, that contribute to the effectiveness of teaching. The total effect can sharpen student motivation, or it can blunt it.

In most of its attributes, the school traditionally has been adjusted to what are defined as normative characteristics of various groups. Often, these norms are more idealistic than realistic. Since they develop over time, are derived from questionable information, and passed by word of mouth, the odds are negligible that they describe the students who are affected by them. Too often, the school is found to be unwilling or unable to bend itself to accommodate to the needs of special groups or of individual students. It is in the matter of motivation that these limitations become particularly troublesome. The student for whom the school has the most positive meaning brings along enough push and pull of one kind or another to sustain him through his daily encounters. His motives are those which keep him in tune with the central theme of the classroom, make him at least minimally responsive to the teacher's guidance, and keep him functioning constructively within a student group.

But many students have motivational characteristics that lead them into conflict with the routine of the school in one way or another. To make their school day a more positive influence would require unusual adaptations on the part of the school itself. It is not enough to expect of a public institution with a critical mission to perform that it serve only half of its population or just those who can adapt easily to its restrictions. Instead, every opportunity must be sought to make education meaningful and desired by everyone. To accomplish this, there must be a program more dynamic and flexible than any program in evidence today. This means that time, space, equipment, supplies, and personnel must be seen in a different light. Despite lip service to the contrary, the tangible elements have determined the program when they should be subordinate to it. Furthermore, the program, instead of being "the thing," must be built upon a set of attainable objectives that have real significance for students of today. It is true that schools are changing and that curriculum reconstruction and other advancements may bring education closer to its potential as a positive force for society.

Since midcentury, we have been in an era marked by rapid and fundamental changes in every aspect of our lives. No institution has been exempt from scrutiny, judgment, and challenge leveled at its role and purpose in the total influence upon the problems of our time. Schools have received an exceptional breadth and depth of concern from both the public and private sectors of society. Unaccustomed to external pressures for change, the institution of education has found itself without a strategy to guide its activity into purposeful and orderly priorities. Commenting on the conditions existing prior to the period when massive urges toward change began, Harold Full (1967) made the following statement:

> Either by its resistance to change or by the ignoring of it, the school seldom really solved or resolved its problems. When changes were made, they were additive by nature—the schools retained everything they were presently engaged in and added a few new ideas, usually in the form of new courses (p. 60).

Many changes have come about in the recent past and, no doubt, many more will occur in the near future. Have these innovations been only window dressing? Or do they really serve to make the school more relevant to the lives of its students?

No school could be more relevant than to bring about major consequences in the motivational aspects of students' lives. Let us examine several components of the school program in terms of motivation and effective teaching. In doing so, the contents of earlier chapters are important to remember because they will help us to keep our minds focused upon students and their motivational qualities. Arbitrary distinctions must be made between curriculum content, school programs, and teacher behavior in the full knowledge that school is an integrated experience. It will help to understand and to emphasize each element as it pertains to motivation if it is considered somewhat independently. Topics to be included in our examination of the school program include: the objectives of the curriculum, content and method, and several innovative programs.

Objectives of the Curriculum

Taking stock of our position in public education, Goodlad (1967) notes the disparity between our awareness of individual differences and our treatment of students. Differences have been disregarded in favor of a set of facts and skills for everyone at prescribed times in their school lives. Teachers, like students, have been constrained by this action. Efforts and energies are absorbed by the task of trying to make a single content understandable and, at the same time, attractive to everyone. Each day, teachers look into the faces of students who they know are not really interested in what is happening to them. Caught without a clear set of purposes as guidelines by which the events of the classroom can be selected, many teachers are confused. In reaction, students become more apathetic or show other forms of avoidance behavior.

It is imperative that the real objectives we seek in education be made clear to teachers and to students. The search for a perfect curriculum seems to have ceased. In reality, no agreement has been reached, nor is it likely to be decided that a given set of experiences can serve the needs of everyone. A casual look at schools reveals that curricula vary extensively. Why, then, shouldn't the curriculum vary from child to child in the same classroom? The answer must be that it should if more will be accomplished by the student. But there must be some logic and purpose behind what teachers and students do in school. What we need and must have is a set of goals specific enough to be understandable and, at the same time, general enough to be applicable. It would improve matters if the goals were phrased in terms of what students are expected to do following a period of schooling.

A set of six behavioral objectives as the outcomes of education has been proposed by Goodlad (1967):

1. The student will use self-appraisal.
2. The student will rely upon himself.
3. The student will show self-control.
4. The student will show proficiency in fundamental movement skills.
5. The student will evidence effective communication skills.
6. The student will use cognitive behaviors with facility.

Goals like these, while they are too vague to be entirely satisfactory, give a teacher more direction than most sets of objectives do. Furthermore, the stage is set for student development to have a place in the focus of the curriculum.

There is a growing recognition that learning "to think critically" is perhaps the ultimate goal of contemporary education. In its search for objectives, the Educational Policies Commission of the National Education Association (1961) has arrived at a significant statement:

> The purpose which runs through and strengthens all other educational purposes—the common thread of education—is the development of the ability to think (p. 18).

This document goes on to make a point concerning the nature of a curriculum suited to this objective:

> No particular body of knowledge will of itself develop the ability to think clearly. The development of this ability depends instead on methods that encourage the transfer of learning from one context to another and the organization of things learned (p. 18).

Easy as it is to say it, development of the ability to think is a most complex undertaking. If the educational slate were wiped clean and we could begin anew, the problems would be fewer. Instead, an alteration of our course must begin in the contemporary scene. To offer an essay on the topic is not the intention here. It is our desire, however, to examine the contextual limitations that are placed upon student motivation. By their nature, many of the perplexing obstacles to a change of educational goal orientation involve serious hazards to motivation, also. A quick look at them can only help in the understanding of motivation in its school context.

1. Society, educators included, cannot as yet subscribe wholeheartedly to the objective of creating critical thinkers. Free as we like to believe ourselves to be, a thinking person is seen as a threat by those around him. As a motto, it is laudable, but as a "for real" goal, we are not ready to accept it.

2. Students and teachers have operationally defined the role of the student as one of passive, reactive recipient of knowledge. Whether the role can be altered for everyone, and how it can be done effectively, are questions needing answers.

3. As philosophers, scientists, artists, and technologists, we have only vague opinions and contradictory theories about thinking. Unable to define it, we are not sure what happens organically, psychologically, or socially when a person uses thought.

4. Relationships among knowledge, values, wishes, emotions, and motives as inputs for the thought process are not clear to us. And yet, if we elect to deal with thinking as a process, we cannot accept responsibility for knowledge and exclude all other inputs.

5. We know something about observable behavior, but in truth, we know little, if anything, about how the ability to think develops.

It is apparent that schools will not become "thought-centered" overnight, in view of these obstacles. It is a fact, however, that a definite movement is under way to increase the emphasis upon thinking in the school life of students. Teachers who subscribe to this doctrine should not apologize for the selection of a curriculum content suitable for individual learners. Neither should they shrink from the initiation of activities that involve students in problem-solving, decision-making, goal-selection, and other motivating pursuits.

Content and Method

We have noted in earlier chapters that there are many conditions in the learner that help to determine his behavior. We are at the point now of dealing with the role of content and instructional method as they relate to student motivation. Today more than ever before, there is a recognition that learning content, teaching method, and student motivation are intimately interwoven. In fact, the relationships are close enough to complicate any attempt to discuss and understand all of the facets. To simplify matters, let us first examine the lowest or first-order relationships that are easily shown in the following conditions:

1. Topics and subjects have varying levels of appeal. Age, sex, and social background of students help to predict the level of appeal or interest.

2. Instructional methods, quite apart from content, have qualities that capture the enthusiastic involvement of certain students and turn others off.

3. Subjects, topics, and skills accommodate to certain teaching methods better than to others.

Combining these simple conditions leads to the conclusions that:

1. Interesting topics taught in interesting ways produce maximum student motivation.

2. The appeal of a topic may be increased by teaching it with a technique known to have motivating potential with students.

3. Uninteresting topics presented in unappealing ways will attract few students.

Simple and obvious conditions of this nature, important as they are, require little or no discussion. Instead, we must concern ourselves with ways teachers can manipulate content and method to maximize student involvement and learning.

National curriculum study groups in science and mathematics have achieved improvement in making their subjects more attractive. While making substantive changes in content, they have accomplished another change that is equally noteworthy. They have built into their content an appealing methodology. Students have been given more time to handle and manipulate equipment and ideas. Following periods of manipulation, students observe and record the consequences of their actions. More recently, the trend toward similar change is occurring in the social studies. Real issues are being discussed in class, and motivation is elevated through student involvement. Unfortunately, the new curricula have been placed in the hands of teachers who have failed to appreciate the value of the discovery method, and its effect has often been lost.

Curiosity, exploration, and manipulation are the natural behaviors with which children are endowed to help them discover their world. Motivated by these action tendencies, children seek out the order and pattern of objects and events they encounter. It is easy to find agreement that we fail to capitalize on this, the most important positive motive children possess. And yet we continue in our tradition as though it made no difference. Does this mean that we deliberately seek to block curiosity? If so, there are several effective ways to go about it. Marx and Tombaugh (1967) list ten ways, and three of them pertain to the content of the curriculum:

1. Deprive students of sensorimotor and verbal stimulation.

2. Overemphasize purely rote learning of uninteresting material without adequate interpretation, explanation, or effort to arouse the child's interest.

3. Present material on a level which the child cannot understand (p. 212).

To their list, many other somewhat more subtle ways can be added:

1. Refrain from the use of novelty material since children tend to become enthralled in it.

2. Do not select subject matter that conflicts with what the student already thinks. Make sure that no elements within the subject content conflict with each other. Thus, we can be certain that it will be easily consumed and forgotten.

3. Select reading matter that contains characters and content with which the student cannot identify.

4. Allow no switching from one book to another, or from one topic to another, because this change will tend to dispel boredom.

5. Select content with few, if any, interesting pictures, diagrams, cartoons, and designs, because students will spend too much time looking at them and miss all the important knowledge.

6. Select books and reference materials that make every point perfectly clear with long, boring, detailed explanations. Then the student will find it unnecessary to think for himself. If he misses one of the points or goes off into a tangent of self-directed thinking, call his attention to what he is missing.

7. Make sure that the student understands clearly what he is to seek when he opens his book. Tell him what he will find, because this robs him of the surprise and, at the same time, convinces him that his teacher knows his stuff.

8. Select reading and study material that employs very bland language, a lot of formality, and many words that are outside the normal vocabulary of the student.

9. Never allow the student to find and use materials of his own selection. The really important facts may not be there, or if they are, they are likely to be phrased in such a way as to confuse him when he takes the test.

10. Beware of the student who gets hung up or shows too much interest in one topic of study. His personal pursuit of greater depth in a particular topic will prevent him from advancing along the broad academic front that the curriculum requires.

There are many other ways to stifle curiosity, but they are discussed in the context of teacher behavior in the next chapter.

Structure of Learning Material

Everywhere, there is a growing awareness of the structure of knowledge as it pertains to subject matter and to student motivation. In the writings of Bruner (1960, 1961, 1964), Ausubel (1960, 1963a, 1965), and many others, we find emphasis upon the organization and meaning of knowledge as significant variables in the learning behavior of students. Scholars urge that the structure and method of each discipline be stressed in the school curriculum (National Education Association 1962). And there is recognition that knowledge, when it is acquired, is organized by the learner into what is called a *cognitive structure.* New knowledge can be taken in (learned) only in relation to relevant concepts, information, and understanding already possessed. At any given point in time, these cognitive materials exist in the mind of the learner in certain relational patterns. The structure of each pattern is determined by whatever meanings have been attached to the bits of material incorporated. Meaning, in this sense, as defined by Weir (1965) is "... the order imposed upon experience by the individual as he becomes aware of the interrelationships between the self and the phenomena encountered in his experience" (p. 281). These meanings as they are organized constitute the cognitive structure which is always in a state of change and development.

In teaching, we are constantly involved with the development of cognitive structures. To accomplish this with efficiency, we must have more than an academic knowledge of the concept of cognitive structure. As teachers become involved with cognitive structures, they must be sensitive to the interaction between the cognitive organization of the learner's present knowledge and the structure of the knowledge to be acquired. When a new learning experience is encountered, the outcome derives in large part from the interaction of two conditions:

(1) the status of the student's cognitive structure to acquire the new learning; and

(2) the organization of the new material to attract and satisfy the learner.

Under ideal conditions, each learning experience should merge with the next to form a complete process. Even a casual examination tends to reveal that, in reality, this is not the case. Continuity in student learning is difficult to guarantee and comes only after concentrated efforts on the part of the teacher.

Why do students evidence unevenness and dissonance in what they learn? For a start, we can admit that a very large part of what we call student learning is not related to meaning. It is rote learning, not because the teacher intends it to be, but for other reasons. Sounds that say a definition, explain an event, describe a situation, or detail an operation are memorized and, for a short time, can be repeated more or less on demand. Because the meanings have not really been acquired, the sounds are soon lost. Visual images of words, designs, maps, and other stimulus materials pass away for the same reason. In other words, content acquired in this form is not fitted into the cognitive structure on any permanent basis. It clings only as superficial or peripheral material which could become integrated into the pattern only with some special attention. Teachers depend too much upon the student to do the integrating in a silent and motionless fashion. Instead, by saying, writing, or in some way applying the material along with cognitions already present, the student is most able to make meanings become evident to himself. Left unattached in terms of meanings, the new material seems to fade away, possibly to be recalled, understood, and applied later, but the risk that this will happen is too great.

Thus, in our haste to teach a great deal of material, we sacrifice much of it to permanent loss, and we create poor learning habits for students. More than this, we rob them of the joy they could acquire from meaningful learning. One job for the teacher, then, is the skillful use of experiences that will prepare the learner to learn new material because he understands and can apply his earlier knowledge.

Preparing the Learner

One approach to preparing the learner to relate meaningfully to new material is described and tested by Ausubel (1960). He prepared learners by presenting to them a set of concepts appropriate and relevant to the learning of new and unfamiliar material. He called these concepts "advance organizers." Learning of the advance organizers improved learning and retention of new materials which we take as evidence that the new material, as a consequence of deliberate preparation, had more meaning for the students. A similar outcome was found by Schuck (1969) who referred to his approach as "set induction." One group of teachers was given special training to prepare them to develop "sets" in students prior to the presentation of new material. Later, students of the teachers who used the set induction techniques (experimental group) were compared with students who had not been exposed to these techniques (control group). Interesting outcomes are reported. Students in the experimental group achieved at significantly higher levels and had better recall of the subject matter. Students rated the teachers who had been given special training as the most effective.

In two experimental studies, we have seen the value of set induction or advance organizers in improving learning of subject matter. In a study reported by Siegel and Siegel (1965), evidence of another kind is shown. They induced in one group a "conceptual set" and in another group a "factual set." It was found that students with the set to learn concepts were adversely affected by emphasis on facts. Conversely, students who were prepared to learn facts were handicapped by the teacher's emphasis upon concepts. Thus it is evident that the "set" employed by the teacher must be logically related to the learning it is designed to improve. Specific suggestions for inducing "sets" are presented in the discussion of teacher behavior in the next chapter.

The "organizing center," as discussed by Goodlad (1962) and Herrick (1968), is a concept that allows for individual differences among learners in a way that will increase motivation. Regardless of the success of efforts at set induction, each student comes into the new learning experience with a unique cognitive structure. New material, to be of maximum interest and suitability for each student, then, must have a complex organization. An "organizing center" is the large topical umbrella that covers a body of learning content much in the way a unit on "transportation" might be conceptualized. Ideally, such centers of organization should provide:

(1) many levels at which students can approach the subject matter;

(2) many kinds of student responsive behaviors involved in its methodology;

(3) the possibility to move in many directions away from it; and

(4) very simple to quite complex organizational aspects within it.

When these qualities are present and evident to each learner, we can anticipate increased interest. Each student should be encouraged to make contact with the material at his unique level of understanding. His own background of experience makes the learning of whatever has meaning for him a unique possibility. Different perceptions occur, and the variety in a single class is amazing. That each student make a response in terms of his own awareness is a necessity. Overt responses are more effective for young, apathetic, and low-motivated students (Rippey 1965). For most students, the overt response that is easiest to make is to say something. If they can talk about what they find in the learning event, the experience is made richer and more personal. This, in addition to intensifying individual enthusiasm, has the advantage of broadening the base of knowledge and insight for everyone. As different thoughts emerge, they stimulate further thought and discussion. It is common to find several fortuities growing out of this happening:

1. Teachers gain insight concerning personality variables, levels of student comprehension, expressive abilities, and interests of individual students.

2. Thoughts and perceptions of the common topic begin to fall into patterns that the students will recognize and discuss.

3. Students and the teacher may develop new respect for the ideas of a student whose contribution stands out.

4. Students who see no joy in dealing with the duller aspects of the topic may find an interesting facet they would otherwise have missed.

5. New thoughts may emerge and lead to further pursuits by the class or by a subgroup.

The so-called "knowledge explosion" has generated new concepts about the nature of the various disciplines. One of the most significant implications of this change is the fact that we can never again consider any discipline as being independent from all others. This observation is most clearly shown in contemporary views about social studies. In his discussion of opinions concerning interdisciplinary learning in social studies, Chatterton (1969) makes a point relating to motivation. He has observed that when elements of two or more subjects are brought together, students showed increased interest. Subjects previously seen as entities somewhat in isolation when they are brought together, create a measure of potential conflict. Students become interested in seeing how the conflict will be resolved. Too often, the teacher resolves this conflict by "telling," thus robbing the enthusiastic student of the pleasure he would get in resolving it for himself. While interdisciplinary teaching finds an obvious base in social studies content, it can be applied in other areas also. We could expect increased student interest in any well-planned effort to combine areas of thought.

Teachers can find ingenious ways to integrate material, to make it interesting, and to involve student action in the learning process. A few examples have been selected to illustrate different applications of concepts already discussed.

A unique approach is described by Clarke (1969) in an article entitled *Simulation for Stimulation.* A political convention was simulated by a whole school in a major effort to substitute action for words and to produce student involvement. Important to note, also, is the careful attention given to evaluation of the project. It was found in the follow-up investigation that the project objectives had been attained. Increases in motivation, involvement, and achievement at all ability levels were evident in students.

It is not unusual to find a school printing a newspaper. Neither is it uncommon for teachers to use commercial newspapers to supplement teaching content. One class combined the two approaches, studying newspapers to learn about all the content areas included, then publishing their own weekly newspaper. Motivation was excellent, and students improved in achievement, thus attaining all objectives for which the project had been intended (Krich 1963).

A much different kind of project is described by Richter (1962). A fresh approach to a library program was based on the deep immersion principle of the "method" school of acting. Interest in library work intensified as a result of the program. The literature of education frequently contains reports of projects like these, and teachers who seek new ways to motivate their students should find such suggestions helpful.

Another way that has been found to increase motivation and improve learning is to approach subject matter, not as a total class, but in smaller groups. There are many ways to divide topics and to create subgroups in a class.

A method that is gaining in popularity is sometimes referred to as *team learning.* Although the technique must take a variety of forms from place to place, certain common characteristics remain evident. First referred to as team learning by Graffam (1964), the approach, as he describes it, has these qualities:

(1) emphasizes the creative development of social and cognitive abilities; and

(2) recognizes that growth through individual effort can be augmented through group processes.

As Graffam used the technique, certain class objectives were selected as appropriate for subgroups to seek on their own initiative. Each team elected a leader or chairman. As part of their learning, each group produced a tangible product relating to its particular body of content and its objective. At the end of the experience, all members of the team received identical marks. The fourth grade of one school used team learning extensively (Poirier 1967). The experience was found to have a liberating influence on students. Their attitudes toward school became more positive.

Motivation tends to improve when students are given opportunities to select what they want to learn and are given the responsibility to pursue their objectives by their own methods. Tasks that are chosen tend to retain their favorable qualities, or even to become more attractive, even though some failure is experienced. Assigned tasks often become less attractive in the face of difficulty (Greenbaum, Cohn, and Krauss 1965).

Interest in school learning is increased when students help others to learn (Hipple 1969; Driscoll 1969). Schools are finding that large-scale involvement of students helping at all levels below their own grade placement is an effective technique for improving motivation. Both the helped and the helper are brought into more intimate contact with the material to be learned. Communication of the learning content to the learner stands to be improved through the use of student-oriented language which teachers may be unable to use very effectively. Both students tend to acquire a sense of responsibility not generally seen in activities involving an entire class or even a small group. Subject matter gains a new value as the medium through which an intimate interaction between two students takes place. While there are hazards inherent in such projects, it is difficult to identify them precisely. Each experience is different and encounters its own set of complications.

Perhaps the most common technique teachers use to stimulate motivation with content material involves working with one student at a time. Individual requirements of one kind or another lead to the selection of a personalized approach to working with a student. It may be the selection of easier and more interesting reading, leading a child to explore his individual interest quite apart from the routine of the class, allowing a pupil to prepare and report on a topic he brings up, or suggesting enrichment topics to be selected by students who want to pursue them. We know that students tire of the usual, the routine, and that they enjoy a change. And research has shown us that feelings of success relate closely with the preferences students have for certain topics (Inskeep and Rowland 1965). A massive enrichment program for all fifth and sixth grade students is described by Remavich and Zilinsky (1963). As a part of his regular school day, each student was allowed to select from several possible areas of enrichment. Students reported that learning was more interesting and more exciting under these special conditions.

Innovative Programs

Continuing to think about school motivation, let us turn our attention to educational change. Underlying most of the innovations we see around the country is a common attempt to take student needs into account. In each program, then, we can expect to find elements that increase student enthusiasm. We have already seen that change in and of itself has a motivating effect. Obviously, space allows us to consider only a selected few of the most popular and noteworthy developments. We must keep in mind, also, that our purpose is to focus upon program elements which stand out by having a significance in motivation.

Earlier Programs

Elective courses, tracks, readings, and honors courses are a few of the earlier efforts to accommodate to student interests and needs. Down through the years, however, the amount of freedom allowed to students in selecting a program has tended to vary. High schools have been victims of the changing pressure from colleges to require certain high school courses. Recent years have brought the requirements for more science, mathematics, and foreign language—a fact that has forced many students away from the creative and performing arts, home economics, shopwork, and the like. This condition, together with increased pressure for high grades, may have produced the findings reported by the Purdue Opinion Panel's survey of a representative sample of adolescents (Leidy and Starr 1967).

1. There is a noticeable decline in students' enjoyment of school.
2. Students want more involvement in school matters.
3. Students want considerably more freedom to decide things for themselves.

This movement, of course, is most in evidence on college campuses. As a result of student dissatisfaction, colleges are reexamining their general education requirements. That students have the power to affect the school's program is evident in the trend toward Black Studies programs in colleges and in an increasing number of high schools. Students have even demanded and have been given remedial services to prepare them for academic life.

The practice of dividing the curriculum of the secondary school into three or more tracks has become a common aspect of many schools. Three usual programs are: vocational, general, and college preparatory. Originally intended to serve the needs of more students efficiently, the track plan has failed in many instances to accomplish its purpose. A diversity of problems has arisen:

1. Students and parents find it very difficult to make decisions that have such far-reaching consequences. Election of a complete curriculum at one time and so early in the life of the student became an

insurmountable problem. Guidance techniques have not been sufficiently helpful.

2. Social stigma have become attached to certain tracks and have assumed influence over student choices.

3. Initially, schools maintained rigorous control and strongly resisted the efforts of students to cross boundaries between tracks. There is a growing tendency to relax these boundaries and to allow more flexibility.

Advanced Placement Programs initiated in 1954 have grown to large proportions. By 1964, more than 2000 high schools were offering courses carrying college credit in 888 colleges (College Entrance Examination Board 1964). In many schools, these programs have dried up the supply of students for readings and honors courses. This is unfortunate because the values of each are different. Perhaps new forms of voluntary study and independent study will provide students the chance to investigate topics of interest and to pursue them with a sense of personal responsibility.

Nongraded (Continuous Progress) Programs

A movement toward nongraded programs, begun during the first quarter of this century, has experienced rapid growth in the past two decades. Initially conceived as suitable for the elementary school, these programs are now being adapted and applied in secondary schools, also. In the following quotation, Goodlad (1965) captures the theme of the nongraded school:

> ... the proper question to ask in starting a child off on his school career is not, "Is this child ready for school?" but "What is this child ready for?" This is the most pregnant idea and is, indeed, at the heart of nongrading (p. 57).

It is necessary, in order to accommodate to this idea, to bring about massive changes in the school itself. Changing the name of a group from "first grade" to "Miss Smith's room" is not enough. As Goodlad's statement implies, the school must be prepared to take the child with whatever readiness he possesses. Then it must build a program wherein he will make continuous progress toward whatever potential goals await him. It is not difficult to see that an ordinary elementary school would be poorly equipped to meet this objective.

Our interest here does not allow us to describe the characteristics of a nongraded school program. Instead, we are concerned with those components that relate to student motivation. At least four extremely important elements relate directly to this topic:

1. New expectations are held for the child. In a graded school, the child is expected to move successfully into and through a prescribed

curriculum at an established rate of speed. More realistic expectations characterize nongrading. The child is expected to accomplish tasks as well as he can, to develop skills as rapidly as he reasonably can, and to move through the school's program, achieving at his optimum rate.

2. Children find increased opportunities to develop positive feelings about themselves. Continuous progress, regardless of rate of achievement, implies success. Instead of large numbers of children having to learn to live with failure, there is pleasure associated with success and achievement. Thus, an anticipation of success is built and this, in turn, builds future success and self-confidence. In our discussion of achievement motivation, the negative effects of a failure orientation were evident.

3. Emphasis is placed upon intrinsic rewards of achievement rather than upon extrinsic reinforcements. Children's achievements are measured in terms of goals attained rather than of their position with respect to a norm or standard. The child is assessed against the learning material and not against other learners. The fact that the child's and the teacher's attention is focused on material and goal attainment constitutes intrinsic reinforcement.

4. Most nongraded programs require the student to make frequent changes from room to room, teacher to teacher, and group to group. These changes lighten the day, increase interest, relieve tension, and generally improve motivation for most students.

While nongrading is taking root and spreading in high schools, the trend is not sweeping the country. Enthusiastic reports come from several places where wholehearted efforts have developed. There is no better spokesman for nongrading in high school than B. Frank Brown (1963) whose writing served as the primary source for the comments here. In addition to the elements listed as characteristic of elementary programs, two others are found in high schools:

1. Students move away from rote learning and simplified explanations and involve themselves with the process of inquiry. (More discussion of the motivational values of discovery learning follows in another section.)

2. Students are given more than ordinary responsibility for their own learning. This draws upon the competence motive proposed by White (1959) and discussed earlier.

Of all the innovations to be developed to the present time, there is little doubt that nongrading is the most radical in its impact. Schools that undergo an immersion in the philosophy and psychology of nongrading find themselves thoroughly revitalized. Teachers become more enthusiastic and find teaching a greater joy. An aura of excitement begins to pervade the school and, for a time at least, wonderful things seem to happen. Despite the fact that scientific evaluations fail to reveal consistently measurable advantages, few observers and fewer participants remain skeptical of the value of nongrading.

Team Teaching

Another innovative movement with a vast implication for motivation is team teaching. Our intent here is to point out and briefly to discuss these motivational components. Readers who seek descriptions of the characteristics of a team teaching program are referred to the works of Trump (1965), and Shaplin and Olds (1964). Like other educational changes, team teaching takes a variety of forms when local faculties express their individualities. This flexibility is an inherent asset of the technique, but it creates problems when we attempt an analysis. Because of this, our discussion will fail to mention valuable components of some projects and will deal with elements not seen in others.

Complete projects of team teaching involve more than a division of the faculty into teams of two or more teachers. The changes wrought in a school are extensive. As each of the following motivational factors is discussed, the impact of these changes should become apparent:

1. Student interest and enthusiasm are intensified by the addition of a new dimension of instruction. Teachers who are afforded the opportunity to deal with their specialties do so with zeal and insight which are contagious to students and fellow teachers. More topics and interesting sidelights are included because teacher time is efficiently scheduled, thus allowing time for embellishments.

2. Ordinarily, because teacher-aides relieve the teacher of routine chores, he has more time for contact with students. A problem of which educators have been aware for many years is the abbreviated amount of time students have for personal contact with teachers. At the same time, we know that motivation is intensified when the learner can shed his cloak of anonymity and assume a significant place in the teacher's actions. Weaknesses in basic skills, communication, and understanding can be overcome, thus helping students to gain new feelings of adequacy. Closer personal contact helps the teacher to know and understand the needs of students which, in turn, provides a base for improving instruction and motivation.

3. Community resource persons may enliven the treatment of a topic by their participation as team members. Use of community consultants is by no means exclusive to team teaching projects. There is, however, a quality in the atmosphere created by teaming, a quality that seems to cause teachers to look more appreciatively at the contributions of others, both fellow teachers and consultants. Students, also, tend to

respond with more than ordinary ardor when outside specialists meet with them. It is not uncommon to see the lazy and apathetic student come to life when someone not directly associated with the school starts to interact with the class.

4. It is usual to find in team teaching frequent and well-planned use of technical aids. In a later chapter, the importance of media in motivation is discussed. It is sufficient to note here that team teaching projects seem to incorporate the best examples of teaching with technical equipment and specially prepared instructional materials.

5. One facet of a well-executed program is the variation of group size for particular activities and topics. This provides stimulation while solving a difficult problem of facility for communication. By employing large group techniques of instruction when it is suitable, time and facilities are made available for small group meetings. In the more intimate circumstance, communication is improved. Students talk more and interact with each other on related topics; teachers listen more and thereby learn more about students. According to Kelicker (1966), small groups produce more creativity in student responses, and teachers carry out more functions associated with effective teaching. Obviously, if these conditions exist, we can assume that students will become more avid participants in the learning process and that they will find increased pleasure from their involvement.

6. It is expected that within the team teaching organization, time and facilities will be set aside for independent learning. If this is accomplished, each student has an opportunity to develop a sense of responsibility for his own learning and a feeling of satisfaction when he achieves a goal. Most traditional instruction robs the student of these feelings that are indispensable in the development of motivation that continues beyond the years of academic life.

7. The last factor, but by no means the least important, is the evaluation of instructional effectiveness by the team itself. As a part of the routine of planning sessions, team members periodically or continually evaluate their performance. Awareness of their strengths and weaknesses certainly must contribute to constant improvement. More importantly, the criterion of effectiveness most likely to be used is the success of the team's efforts in getting students interested and involved in the learning program. Thus, motivation becomes a central issue around which the entire team effort is developed.

Grouping and Group Influences

To group or not to group has been a perplexing problem for educators for several decades and is a problem that will likely be with us for some time to come. Grouping, as it is used here, refers to some approach to clustering students in a way that produces more homogeneity than would result from a randomized assignment to classes. The most frequently used criteria are the results of achievement and intelligence tests, along with the recommendations of teachers and counselors. Assessments of the effectiveness of various techniques of grouping are frequent in educational literature, and one can find support or lack of it for almost any viewpoint (Franseth 1963; Jones 1966). Those who have looked deepest into the problems associated with evaluation of grouping practices note that when significant differences are shown, they favor the most able students at the expense of those of lower ability. Less able students may miss the stimulation produced by the more able students (Jones 1966). Cawelti (1963) reports that, while there is general satisfaction with the results of well-developed grouping practices, high school teachers find trouble motivating low and average groups.

One of the most extensive studies of ability grouping was carried out by Walter R. Borg (1966) who studied more than 2500 students in Utah. His numerous findings cannot be covered here except to a limited degree. Data covered the range from fourth through twelfth grade. He concluded that:

1. Achievement of elementary school pupils was not significantly higher in ability grouping.

2. There was a tendency for superior-ability students to show greater gains in arithmetic and for average students to gain more in science when they were ability-grouped in junior high school.

3. Ability-grouped students were more often classed as overachievers.

4. Students in randomly-grouped classes developed better study habits in elementary school.

5. Ability grouping did not rob average- and low-ability groups of leadership.

6. Student problems were fewer in grouped classes in junior and senior high schools.

7. Placement of a student into a lower-ability group tends to depress his self-concept and self-acceptance. On the other hand, a personality inventory failed to reveal feelings of inferiority in low-ability groups.

Regardless of our personal views about grouping, we still face the fact that students spend their hours at school in one kind of group or another. Only infrequently does the choice of a group fall to the student. We have failed to give serious consideration to this problem of school organization despite our full awareness of its significance.

Groups have strong influences upon the feelings and behaviors of constituent members. Why is this true? Because man has an apparent need to affiliate with others—people need people. The individual, at times, is willing and anxious to give up his autonomy and to follow the will of others in order to be an accepted member of a group. A fascinating body of literature has been developed by the report of research and theory relating to group functions, but there is not space here to deal with it. Its importance for teachers who work with groups constantly must be recognized, and they are urged to become more knowledgeable and skillful by their own inquiry.

There is a viewpoint, and it is strongly supported, that the peer group influence upon high school students is a deterrent to school objectives. Coleman (1961), in his research on this matter, found that students in elite, or leadership, roles held the school and scholarly activity in low regard. He noted, too, that athletes were more popular than scholars. The same, or similar, findings have been reviewed by Boocock (1966) who formulated two hypotheses that relate to peer acceptance and school learning:

1. On the basis of security and acceptance in interpersonal relationships, a student will have a positive attitude as well as freedom from conflict, and therefore, he will be better able to learn.

2. Achievement may be a compensation for failure and rejection in social relations; thus school learning may be hindered by strong group satisfactions.

Let us examine these two viewpoints in more depth. At issue are the conditions necessary for academic achievement. The first proposition is built upon the concept that until an individual's need for security and acceptance has been satisfied, he cannot devote his energies to cognitive materials. Maslow (1954) supports this position, as noted earlier, by placing man's needs in a hierarchy constructed on the contention that progress from a lower to a higher order need depends upon adequate satisfaction of the needs that are most basic. He places *belongingness* at the third level, beneath *esteem, self-actualization,* and *aesthetic needs* which are at the fourth, fifth, and sixth levels, respectively. Speaking to the Nebraska symposium on motivation, Maslow (1955) described the self-actualizing person as sometimes showing no need for people and even feeling hampered by them. His explanation of what might appear to be an inconsistency between these two thoughts would, of course, be that the person's belongingness needs were filled by a small amount of acceptance and love.

There is some evidence that feelings of adequacy, belongingness, and esteem may not be necessary for high achievement need. As noted earlier, Martire (1956) found students with the highest achievement motive to feel considerable dissatisfaction with themselves. The theory of cognitive dissonance as proposed by Festinger (1957, 1968) is built upon the proposition that energy for achievement comes from discord and conflict. Compensation has been an accepted mechanism in psychology for generations, and it remains in evidence in human behavior as it relates to achievement in school.

What, then, are the relationships among satisfaction of the need for affiliation, group influences upon behavior, and academic motivation? To say that they are simple and direct would be to ignore the complexities of human behavior and of group dynamics and influence. Individuals have multiple needs which are not always in accord. What satisfies one need may serve to postpone or deny gratification of another. For example, a student with high need for achievement will find that to affiliate with or to be placed in a group where achievement is taboo requires him to make a decision. If his need to achieve outweighs his need for acceptance in the group, he is most likely to work and to live with the resulting rejection. A much more frequent case is the student who elects to go along with the crowd and forego or postpone his need for achievement. Clarke (1962) and Nash (1964) found that underachievers seek peer-group acceptance and social relationships to the extent that this takes precedence over academic pursuits. Also, it was found by Granzow (1954) and by Kurtz and Swenson (1951) that in grades four to six, at least, underachievers had fewer friends, and the attitudes of their friends toward academics were less positive than were the attitudes of achievers' friends.

Another kind of situation is encountered by the student whose need for achievement is low but who finds himself in a group where achievement is held in high regard. To attain status in the group, he must work for achievement. If he sees the others in the group being rewarded, he is likely to imitate their behaviors (Clark 1965). Assuming he has the ability to achieve success for himself, the group influence will have helped him to develop a stronger need for achievement while he is satisfying his affiliation needs. The effects of imitative behavior must not be discounted in motivation. Parents and teachers are not quick to realize that children tend to imitate what they see rather than what they are told to do. This fact makes the influence of the group an all-powerful one in the school life of the child.

A student who finds that he cannot achieve the success demanded by the group faces a serious problem. If he is unable to escape from the group, or if he has an intense need for affiliation, he is ripe for appeal to the baser needs of the group as a clown, a goat, or a servant for the leadership. Teachers see this develop often but can do nothing about it if the student is forced to remain where he is. Of course, the student has other alternatives. He can withdraw, become hostile, or resort to any of a variety of other behaviors.

Groups exercise an influence toward uniformity (Festinger 1954). Whether or not an individual bends with that pressure is a matter of question. In general, the influence of the group can be viewed as a crucial factor, an "acid test" in bringing an individual to a decision point in his own behavior. This means that the student whose inclinations are contrary to the direction taken by the group's pressure must either resist its influence or conform to it. Resistance may cause enough arousal in the individual to thrust him beyond the success or failure levels he would otherwise reach. If he conforms, the outcome depends upon a complex of interrelated variables. Ordinarily, conformity strengthens behavior tendencies.

Let us examine two group characteristics to determine a few of their implications for motivation. Without doubt, the most influential qualities of group behavior are cooperation and competition.

Cooperation — Competition: Our era has seen an intense effort to replace academic competition with cooperation. Kilpatrick, an eminent authority on education philosophy appropriate for our changing society, made a strong plea for an emphasis upon cooperation (Frankel 1965). His desire was to make school experience a center for active, energetic, youthful purpose based upon each member's cooperative contribution to the larger interest and welfare of the group. Other pressures have sought to maintain competition as the child's preparation for a world of business and other elements of a competitive society. Persons who seek to maintain a competitive atmosphere in the classroom claim that it arouses motivation and provides an incentive for those who excel. Those who push for cooperation claim much the same advantage but place the glory of achievement in terms of team effort and acclaim. It is the view of Frankel (1965) that neither competition nor cooperation is bad in its own right.

Competition, without doubt, can be a stimulus to achievement if the conditions are right. If the participants feel they have a chance to win or to make a good showing, they will compete. Rote learning for short periods of recall has been found to respond most favorably to competition. Negative effects of competition have been well described by Weinberg (1965). He points out that intense anxiety created by the fear of failure is aroused by highly competitive conditions. This anxiety then leads to a reaction against the school, the teachers, and possibly against society, in Weinberg's opinion.

Children seem naturally to seek competition whether or not it is created for them. We do not have the evidence as yet to know how early in life competitiveness appears, but we know that by the time they are eight years of age, most children show signs of it in several dimensions of their behavior. In a study not as yet published, the writer investigated the competitiveness of children from two ungraded elementary schools and two schools with traditional graded programs. All four student groups came from middle-class neighborhoods. The mean scores for children in their third, fourth, fifth, and sixth years of school attendance did not differ significantly. Neither did the mean scores for any of the four groups favor either a graded or an ungraded school. Thus it appears that the nature of the ungraded school fails to have the effect of reducing the competitive attitudes of children. If children have an inherent need to match their performance against others, as seems to be the case, it remains for the school to take full, but wise, advantage of it. To avoid the ill effects, we must prevent children from facing frequent failure by controlling the competition to insure success for everyone. Perhaps these suggestions are in order:

1. As quickly as possible, reorient competition from other persons to a self-established standard of excellence. This can be accomplished by providing circumstances in which each child selects a goal for his own achievement and learns to reward himself for reaching it.

2. Utilize competition between groups or classes and reward all students of the group for their efforts toward attainment of group objectives. It might be stimulating to have a student compete with a matched student in a school geographically isolated from his own. By exchange of photographs and letters, each child could get to know enough about his academic opponent to make the competition interesting. Then if the students were well paired, their success would tend to alternate while isolation would prevent some of the social side effects of competition. It seems important that teachers become more aware of the effects of competition and that they develop skill in the wise use of it.

Effects of cooperation are not as well understood and consequently, they receive less attention by investigators. Superficially, they are all assumed to be desirable, but this may not be true. Children do not move as easily into cooperation as they do into competition. They seem to learn cooperation out of repeated opportunities to function as contributing members of a group. When students cooperate, their reinforcement must come from pride in the group accomplishment. This can be possible only if their own part in the product can be seen as having been an important contribution. Creating the appropriate conditions for cooperation takes planning and thought by the teacher. Here are a few suggestions:

1. **Establish groups small enough to allow each student to be active and to share in the group effort.**

2. **If possible, have each group produce a tangible output to show for its work.**

3. **Establish groups that will as nearly as possible assure a place of importance for each participant.**

4. Avoid having the same leaders take over the groups each time.

5. Maintain a close supervision of group activities in order to sustain the cooperative spirit and to avoid interpersonal conflicts.

6. Give students enough opportunities to function in groups to let them become comfortable at it.

We seem to be entering an era when cooperation for its own value has little appeal to students. They are demanding more individual rights and personal dignity as the price of cooperation. They want to know, also, that the total effort has a purpose which is worthwhile to themselves. Wise application of cooperation as a functional behavior for school accomplishment can help teachers to work effectively with the students of today and tomorrow.

Programmed and Computer-Based Instruction

Two approaches to independent learning have been selected for consideration in this section. While there are similarities between programmed instruction and computer-based instruction, there are a few important differences; therefore, we must treat them separately.

Programmed Instruction: When programming first began to find large-scale acceptance in the schools, many expected it to have a sweeping impact. This has not happened, at least not to the extent of original expectations. We cannot bother ourselves with the possible reasons for this failure but instead, we examine the motivational implications of this technique of learning. Programming of learning content involves several critical operations. The significant highlights of a body of content must be isolated for inclusion in the program. These may be facts, concepts, relationships among critical ingredients, processes, and procedures. After these content elements have been arranged in a logical sequence, each subtopic is broken down into smaller steps which are then phrased as questions. Each tiny step, or frame, is built upon the preceding one, with the gap between them so small that the learner can bridge it without making an error. Frames are then arranged in a format that provides for the student to make an overt response following each question. By one simple operation or another, the learner causes the correct response to appear before him and then moves on to the next frame. Each commercially produced program is tested thoroughly before it is published.

These statements describe what is referred to as a *linear* program. It is designed to stimulate the student to emit the response determined by the subject matter as seen by the author of the program. Each small response is rewarded by immediate feedback when the student is shown the correct answer. Since these programs are built in easy steps which guarantee constant success, it is assumed that the learner gets consistent positive reinforcement.

Another technique is called *intrinsic* or *branch* programming. The differences are essentially these:

1. Frames are arranged so as to give the learner a multiple-choice situation rather than the opportunity for a single fixed answer.

2. The different choices made by students key them to go to different material.

3. A short discussion of the learning content ordinarily is presented just before the question is given.

4. When incorrect alternatives are chosen, the student is directed to a place where the explanation of his mistake is found.

5. Pages of the programmed material are organized randomly, thus forcing a student to do each item before he can know where to go for his next item. Skipping around is made very difficult.

For a more thorough explanation of the differences between intrinsic and linear programming, the reader is referred to Crowder (1963).

Many qualities of programmed instruction are psychologically designed to increase motivation. The system and sequence of the program have an intrinsic value in that students see logical organization and find subgoals that can be identified and attained. A feeling of success has positive value in moving the student forward to future successes. Making an overt response involves the student more actively in the learning process. Feedback of the correctness of a response provides an intrinsic reinforcement that is encouraging.

Branching programs have fewer of these qualities than linear programs do, but they provide for more divergent thinking. Also, more complex material can be handled. Students feel increased responsibility for their choices, and there is more intrigue inherent in the branching approach. Brighter students sometimes become bored with the tiny steps of the linear programs, and they feel underchallenged. Branching programs are constructed in such a way as to present easier or more difficult levels of each concept, depending upon the selection of responses to each multiple-choice item. Thus, students of varying abilities can be expected to find themselves "at home" with the program.

In addition to the inherent motivators, there are other implications. Students enjoy the change provided by their involvement in a new experience. Programmed materials are interesting in their format in that they are somewhat like a puzzle which attracts one until it has become a familiar thing. Being able to move as rapidly as one wishes has a stimulating effect. If the program is controlled by a machine, added incentive is created by the opportunity to manipulate and examine the machinery. However, after a while, these exotic qualities lose their appeal, and teachers find that student motivation in programmed learning has waned. As a full diet, programming has been a disappointment. Its most advantageous use seems to be, for short periods of time, for accelerated study, for making up deficiencies in needed concepts, and for handling a short unit that the teacher either cannot or prefers not to include in the routine of regular instruction. An authority such as Stolurow (1963) feels that programmed learning has a permanent place in the educational program but that its best form has yet to be discovered.

Many qualities of programmed instruction have been incorporated in teaching machines of various types. Their variety and diversity of purpose and function defy description in our limited space. Psychologically, most of them are sound, and few educators can find legitimate criticism on the basis of their effectiveness in instruction. Economically, however, only the simplest are within the budgetary reach of most schools.

Computer-Based Instruction: Certainly, computer-based instruction is expensive, but since it has a lot of versatility, it deserves some attention. A student interacts with a computer in much the same way as he would with a teacher whose full attention could be focussed upon the child's learning.

Typically, the child's name is entered into the computer information at the beginning and is used when the computer addresses him. The amount of student initiative required in a learning sequence can be programmed and modified from one student to the next. Also, the level of difficulty can be varied from one student to another, and for the same student, from one response to the next. Motivation derives from the manipulation of the device, the freshness of the experience, intrinsic qualities of the learning content, and reinforcements given by the computer's reactions to the student's responses. Flexibility which allows the computer to handle various levels of difficulty holds potential for motivating students because their successes can be maximized. Computers can instruct one child, a class, or subgroups within a larger group. Potentials of computers in the instructional process have scarcely been sampled, and the future should see massive involvements, assuming, of course, that the costs can be reduced.

Television Teaching

Both closed circuit and broadcast television in the schools have had a vast impact on students, but television in the home has probably had more influence on them. That television has implications for motivation is obvious. Educational television has fallen short of commercial broadcasting in its ability to arouse people and to have an impact upon their thinking. Chief among the many reasons for this may be the blandness of ETV as compared with commercial productions. Educators seem to hesitate to present content at an intense and emotional level, thus sacrificing the possible motivational effect upon the viewers. In an extensive study of ETV in ninety classrooms in Boston, Garry (1960) found that pupil attitudes did not seem to change as a result of television education despite efforts to bring about change. He found, also, that students of high initial interest and of high measured intelligence lost interest as the year progressed.

Students can find personal involvement in a television learning experience by projecting themselves into it for short periods of time. However, it is difficult to control and predict the extent of student involvement (Jacobs, Grate, and Downing 1963). It was found in the same study that students seemed to tire of TV when it was used extensively.

Used properly, TV can bring into the classroom many stimulants to motivation not available in the immediate environment. To be of maximum benefit, however, the TV experience must be integrated with the regular classroom learnings. Students must have an opportunity to discuss what the TV brings to them, or else, like any other experience, it is likely to be forgotten.

Discovery Learning

Not enough can be said for the motivational effects of well-conducted discovery learning experiences. If our objective in education is to have students develop a love for learning, then we must provide them the guided opportunities to learn for themselves. They must be encouraged to explore, manipulate, inquire, examine, and form conclusions from their findings. Then they must become aware of the importance of testing their formulations, and they must be helped to develop suitable testing techniques. This kind of education capitalizes upon natural curiosity and, at the same time, provides a sense of personal accomplishment. We have already touched on this topic, and it comes to the fore again in our discussion of teacher behavior in the following chapter. Therefore, it is not necessary to dwell on it further at this point.

6

Teacher Influence

Teachers are the most influential determiners of student motivation. For decades, educational leaders have insisted that this is so, but early efforts to study this influence failed to reveal much of real value. Recent investigations have been more fruitful. Now the influence of the teacher and the learning situation may replace methods and materials as the focus of educational research (Bond and Dykstra 1967; Harris 1969). Already there is a large accumulation of information much of which speaks directly to the concerns of this chapter. Readers who wish to pursue the topic more broadly and deeply are referred to Withall (1949), Flanders (1965), Gage (1963), Medley and Mitzell (1958), Amidon and Hunter (1966), and Page (1963).

Left on their own, without a solid theory of instruction to guide them, many teachers have resorted to feeble and futile attempts to encourage motivation. They have told students how important school is, and they have insisted that schoolwork must occupy a large segment of students' lives. Instilling fear, using threats, giving low grades or high grades, sending notes to parents, scolding or resorting to ridicule have been frequent (Gans 1963). According to Hughes (1963), teachers have restricted themselves to a very narrow selection despite the availability of a wide range of behavior. This is not to say that all teachers have performed in such futile fashion. Others have been resourceful and dynamic, using themselves efficiently and effectively. They have performed a wide range of behaviors, from fairly active direct supervision to thoughtful and planned support. They have been able to get obedience from students when it seemed necessary, as well as initiative when it was needed. To perform so effectively requires extraordinary personal qualities.

Good teaching involves more than knowledge of the topic to be learned. On this point, even those authorities with the most divergent views about teaching can agree. However, the search for a description

80

of just what competencies are required has been a long and frustrating one. The fact that no satisfactory list has as yet been proposed is not surprising. Teachers are unalike, and good ones are as different as day and night. They are persons, with all the uniqueness and individuality that could be expected in any profession (Combs 1964). This "person-ness," as Combs refers to it, is the source of whatever commonality exists among good teachers. First of all, they are persons, real and genuine. In the thought of Rogers (1967), "when the facilitator is a real person, being what he really is and entering into a relationship with the learner, without presenting a front as a facade, he is likely to be effec-tive" (p. 45). And it is the totality of the teacher that interacts with students in the school setting, not just his intellect, his physical move-ments, or his personal warmth.

A serious handicap for teachers is that the traditional language of pedagogy attempts to describe a teaching that does not exist. Teachers are said to *impart* knowledge, *involve* the student, *imbue* him with a love of learning, *instill* wisdom, *implant* ideas, *build* concepts, *enlarge* perspectives, and *control* behavior. These words describe activities outside the learner. Learning occurs from within, students involve themselves, learners come to love learning, concepts develop from perceptions, perspectives widen, and behaviors emerge from the learner. When teachers focus their attitudes and actions upon this con-cept of teaching, they begin to see themselves differently. They become instruments, dynamic and influential, whereby the conditions develop to maximize the likelihood that motivation and learning will occur.

Teachers' Perceptions

The way a teacher perceives himself, his students, the subject mat-ter, teaching, and his world shapes his performance. Self-perception is at the center of this complex, and thus it should be considered first. Before a teacher can be the real, genuine person Rogers (1967) dis-cusses, he must accept himself. What does self-acceptance involve? Its basic ingredient is a form of love—a sensing and prizing of one's own worth or value as a human being. Both knowledge and understanding of self are gained from sensitivity to internal forces and to the reactions we stimulate in those around us. Perceiving ourselves as worthy and valuable human beings does not require that we be pleased with our behaviors. Actually, one must be able to deal separately with the self and the deed. This is not as senseless and difficult as it seems if one realizes that the two phenomena come from different levels of the personality. The self as we are able to experience and know it is con-scious and personal. It does not involve external objects or others—only perceptions of them as points of reference.

Behavior, on the other hand, involves the unconscious as well as the conscious coming into real contact with the externals that surround us. Self-accepting teachers are able to experience their own feelings and actions in an objective manner and face up to them. In doing so, they become better able to make modifications as they are indicated. More than this, the self-accepting teacher is free to perceive external objects and other persons with greater objectivity.

A teacher who aspires to be successful with students must first accept them. Accepting others involves all the states described for self-acceptance. Almost magically, when it occurs, it is communicated to the other. Children, particularly, seem to have a sensitivity that tells them whether or not they are accepted. This communication is sublanguage—experienced as feeling—and the child cannot be fooled by words. Interestingly, when this feeling of acceptance exists, it stimulates the receiver to do something positive in return. In school, the reciprocal action most likely will be to try harder and longer, to attend more closely the significant events, and thereby, to learn more efficiently.

What other perceptions lead to good teaching? In his artful description of a perceptual approach to teaching, Combs (1964) lists and discusses several:

(1) rich perceptions about subject matter;
(2) awareness of how things seem to others;
(3) accurate perceptions of people and their behavior;
(4) favorable perceptions of themselves;
(5) clear and accurate perceptions of the purposes and processes of learning; and
(6) realistic perceptions of teaching methods.

Naturally, Combs has hypotheses about what the terms *rich, accurate, favorable,* and *realistic* imply, and readers are urged to pursue his thoughts further. Since virtually the same points have been covered in earlier chapters, they are not repeated here. Instead, our attention turns to the consideration of several dimensions of teacher behavior and motivation.

Teacher Behaviors that Motivate Students

Unless teaching behavior is further segmented, any discussion of it is ambiguous. A practical approach to making this breakdown is to use as a base the chronological sequence through which teaching develops. Despite obvious overlaps and interrelationships between stages, these recognizable sequential behaviors seem to stand out:

(1) selecting and planning learning activities;
(2) making learning objectives known;
(3) preparing students for the new learning;
(4) conducting and reinforcing learning; and
(5) evaluating learning outcomes.

Each step calls for a variety of activity by the teacher, and student motivation is a necessary ingredient at each point along the way.

Selecting and Planning

While the concepts to be learned by students may be structured by the existing curriculum, teachers have freedom to select and plan their own classroom activities. Student interest and participation are the two most vital motivational components available to the teacher in this stage of the teaching sequence. From their general knowledge of children's interests and from observation of students in class, teachers have a good base for designing interesting activities. A few alternatives should be available for individuals with specific needs. Students can be profitably involved in selecting and planning their own activities. Teachers who use their own behavior to stimulate students at this point in the teaching sequence will find several results. Children can be helpful while being original, inventive, and creative. There is evidence that students have a need for activity (Hill 1956). Although there is some necessity for freedom in the satisfaction of this need, freedom should be released, in part, under guided conditions. Participation in decision-making and planning, with the guidance of a teacher, can be a constructive way of satisfying the need for activity.

Children get pleasure and learn a great deal from making the necessary displays, arranging equipment, and attending to other as- [*films*] pects of preparation. Two advantages come from their participation— [*tape*] a closer personal involvement and better understanding of the functions and meanings of each component part in the learning experience being planned. The new activity becomes more than just something happening to them—it assumes a personal significance. More than this, while exploring possibilities, manipulating parts, and organizing them into a meaningful sequence, the student opens up new avenues for learning.

New learning activities should contain several appeals to motivation in order to maximize the impact upon students. A variety of student behaviors should be called for as a means of overcoming boredom, while at the same time, taking individual learning styles into account. Skinner (1968) suggests that "bright colors, variety, sudden change, big type, animated sequences—all these have at least temporary effect in inducing the student to look and listen" (p. 105). Temporary appeal, [*visual*] while it will not carry an experience along to its completion, can serve [*aids,*] to get the attention of students directed toward what is to be learned. At strategic times, introduction of a unique object or event, use of a piece of equipment, or a surprising application of some kind should be included. Motivational value is increased if students are left to find this uniqueness for themselves or, at most, are encouraged to look for it.

Partially concealed but identifiable objects or thoughts have appeal for
the finder. Making them too obvious, however, is likely to destroy the
desired effect.

Teachers are challenged by the necessity to use themselves cre-
atively. At first, they may struggle helplessly to find ways to increase
motivation, but with practice, they improve. As their efforts begin to
pay off, they find that learning sequences develop and progress more
smoothly and that students acquire more learning.

Making Objectives Known

Groping aimlessly through the curriculum or doing what one is
directed to do is not a stimulating and pleasurable way to learn. It is not
surprising that most students tire, "turn off," and fail to develop an
intrinsic motivation for academic learning. A love of learning develops,
not from dependence on the teacher or some other external agent, but
from one's own experiences. At entrance to school, children have a
natural motivation to ask, "Why?" By their own behavior, teachers can
build upon this motive. Children can learn to set goals and standards
for themselves. By the time they are in high school, according to Leidy
and Starry (1967), students want more involvement, and they value a
sense of discipline and responsibility. Teachers have at their disposal
the facilities and opportunities to make school more meaningful. As
models, their own behavior has an influence upon the personal development of students. By their behavior, also, teachers create the circumstances wherein purposeful and responsible behaviors are learned from
successful application.

In the writings of Bandura and Walters (1963) and Grusec and
Mischel (1966), there is evidence that describes the influential value of
models. Research reveals that models who are rewarding, who have
prestige, who show competence, who have status, and who possess
control over the resources of reward are the ones who are imitated.
Teachers have a natural access to the imitative life of the student.
Unfortunately, there are teachers who serve as poor models. One
source of poor modeling is seen in teachers who fail to set objectives and
standards of excellence for themselves and the class. Either too busy,
or simply not aware of its importance, they drift from day to day and
later discover that their students are not with them. Other poor models
are found in teachers who hold objectives for themselves which they
never communicate directly to students. Kept in the lesson planning
book or in the back of the teacher's mind, these goals lose their rightful
impact upon students. Then there are teachers who do not know what
objectives to establish. Their goals tend to be in the nature of work they
expect to finish, such as to show the characteristics of a "set" in mathematics, to acquaint students with the major causes of the American

Civil War, or to complete the unit on transportation. These are plans, whereas objectives ought to involve student accomplishment and be evident in behavior following the learning experience.

Goals and objectives are of sufficient importance to be given a significant place in teaching behavior. This implies that, instead of being left in the background, the act of goal-setting should be made to stand out in the awareness of the student. Everyone should see that the teacher feels this is a real and worthy action to be performed. Then, by means of class discussion, committee work, and individual thought, clearly stated objectives should be developed for every unit of learning. Teachers who have directed their own behavior to shape student goal-setting are likely to observe that:

(1). Students enjoy having a part to play in deciding what they are to achieve.

(2). There is consistent improvement in goal-setting effectiveness as more opportunities are provided.

(3). Students tend to become more realistic in assessing their own potentials for success.

(4). Work intensifies in the pursuit of self-selected goals.

(5). Enjoyment is evident as students achieve what they set out to do.

(6). Students improve in their ability to evaluate their own accomplishments.

There are many other outcomes that help doubtful teachers to increase their faith in the responsible behavior of students. But it must be remembered that goal-setting is a matter of developmental learning, and that the first attempts are likely to be feeble and to show the need for improvement. The payoff is great, however, for teachers who make the effort to shape students in this very important behavior. At the same time, the use of clear objectives improves student performance in a learning episode (Connelly 1956).

Preparing Students for New Learning

In our earlier reference to "set induction," only the cognitive conditioners were mentioned. There are affective elements that have a direct relationship as well. Preparatory actions by teachers can help students to develop several entrance attitudes that will increase motivation. Eagerness to enter the new experience can result from teacher behaviors that hint at mystery, that partially reveal interesting content, that evidence importance of new learnings, and that build the anticipation of success and enjoyment. The actions teachers may use to create these feelings are many, and talking is only one of them. Carefully constructed displays that bring an unfamiliar related object into the classroom, that hint at surprise or mystery, or that show personal eagerness, as well as introducing a variety of other stimulating behaviors, are effective. If the class has helped to select the activity and has developed objectives for themselves, this preparatory stage flows naturally from it and may, in fact, seem to be unnecessary.

Teachers, like coaches, must develop a sense of awareness of when the "learning team" has reached a point of readiness. Coaches plan and devote great care to bringing their athletic teams to a peak of attitude and skill at game time. Athletes are frequently heard to comment that they were, or were not "up" for the game. Because of the fact that some students who are also athletes are aware of this, we can guess that their enthusiasm would not be chilled by their knowing that their teachers use the same tactics. Gamesmanship comes naturally to some teachers but must be learned by others. How effectively teachers can learn to create "upness" in students remains to be seen.

Conducting and Reinforcing Learning

Academic learning has always been looked upon as the focus of the school. It is quite natural, then, that opinions concerning the effectiveness of certain modes of teaching tend to be strong and diverse. There are teachers who feel that the actions of telling, showing, explaining, illustrating, questioning, and assigning are the most effective ways to teach. Others lean toward organizing, suggesting, guiding, stimulating, eliciting, and reflecting as being the most effective methods of teaching. The viewpoint presented here supports the value of the behaviors favored by each group. Used appropriately, each behavior has a positive influence upon motivation and learning. Children, by their natures, expect different behaviors from their teachers. Early experiences in the home and at school help to create tendencies of dependence or independence which, in turn, cause the student to expect certain behaviors on the part of teachers (Jakubczak and Walters 1959). To meet this expectancy and to have some influence in shaping it requires the teacher to use a variety of behaviors while conducting and reinforcing learning.

Creating an appropriate climate for learning is an act of teaching that calls for skill in the use of one's own behaviors. This climate is composed of both affective and cognitive elements closely interwoven and interdependent. Before the atmosphere is created, a decision is necessary. What kind of atmosphere is best for the particular learning task to be most fruitful? Eisner (1963) states a clear case for conceptualizing teacher behavior as the principal influence determining the desired atmosphere. He views the teacher as analogous to an actor who successfully creates a mood in his audience. Acting of this type does not betray one's own genuineness; it simply calls for the ability to use oneself to create different expectancies in students from time to time. This can be done without sham and facade.

An example of the range of behaviors required of a teacher is found in the differences between directed and discovery learning. Both types of learning are important and have rightful places in the life of the student (Craig 1969). Certain tasks call for and most efficiently flow from an atmosphere of attentiveness, quiet listening, following directions, seeing illustrations, and practicing certain operational procedures. An atmosphere of this type is best created by teacher behaviors that:

(1) **call attention to the necessity for this type of learning;**
(2) **promise that it will not last too long;**
(3) **calm the group; and that**
(4) **deliberately and openly deal with the mood-setting problem by getting students to become aware of themselves as they attempt to assume a mood appropriate for the learning experience.**

Students have natural motives of mastery and competence which can be called up to aid them in preparing themselves for a task. Some challenge must be evident, and there must be at least moderate expectancy of success.

Other classroom tasks most effectively develop in an atmosphere of inquiry and active search for knowledge and understanding. Preparing the atmosphere for this approach requires the teacher to provide a model that suggests the proper amount of incongruity (Hunt 1963). What is the proper amount of incongruity for exploration and curiosity to become activated? It must not be so out of reason that doubt and bewilderment are aroused. At the same time, the student must find enough mismatch between existing and potential knowledge to make the exploration interesting. An atmosphere of expectancy can be created by behaviors like these:

(1) **hinting at and toying with the ideas and concepts to be discovered;**
(2) **showing personal enthusiasm;**
(3) **promise of surprise;**
(4) **openly discussing the joy of discovery; and**
(5) **suggestions about the rewards that learning the particular content to be discovered will produce.**

The teacher's role in conducting an inquiry experience has been the topic of several recent writings. Skinner (1968) says "The teacher arranges the environment in which discovery is to take place, he suggests lines of inquiry, he keeps the student in bounds. The important thing is that he should tell him nothing" (p. 109). For readers who wish to pursue this matter further, there are the works of Bruner (1961), Suckman (1961), Schwab (1962), Goodlad (1966), Combs (1966), and many others.

By one or more means, the material to be learned is caused to unfold for the student. Teacher behavior during this unfolding process is critical. Ideally, the teacher shapes his own behavior to the nature of the task. If an active role as a presenter of the learning content is appropriate, the teacher should select behaviors that make a suitable impact on the learner. Usually, telling is not enough. Neither is it sufficient, ordinarily, to direct that students read certain pages in a book. While either of these behaviors has legitimate place in the teaching role, neither should be relied upon too frequently nor for too long a period of time.

variety

Optimum levels of motivation and learning seem to be created by multisensory inputs. The natural need for change and variety applies to the mode of sensory input as well as to content. Students have an ability they often put to use in school. This ability allows the head to be turned toward the source of a sound, the face to assume an expression suggesting some form of intelligence, and the ears to remain open to sound waves. But from this point on, strange things can happen— sounds fade into jumbled and garbled nonsense—visual inputs blur and dance in a psychedelic panorama—and internal meanderings of the mind play undisturbed. Magically, when the lecture ends, the organism returns from its trip, assumes a state of animation, and leaves the classroom relatively untouched. Pulling the shades and closing the doors do not occur so readily when more exciting forms of stimulation are used to carry the message.

An oral description of the Grand Canyon, of a day in court, or of the sweep of barbarian hordes upon Rome fails to make the maximum impact. Seeing slides, motion pictures, or some other form of projection not only is a stronger stimulus, but conveys a broader communication. Almost any student—even the unmotivated—derives some learning from this expansive visual experience.

A very subtle condition, one not often encountered in the literature of education, seems to add still another dimension to communication by visual media. One student, when asked to express his reactions to a closed-circuit TV lesson in social studies, provided an insight that startled the writer. Asked whether he learned the same amount, more, or less, than he would have learned in a personal classroom encounter with the teacher and the lesson, the student replied "much more." To the question "Why do you feel this way?" he made his reply: "While viewing a TV lesson or a movie in class, I feel an urgency to catch everything that happens. I know I can't have a second chance to see it or hear it. When the teacher is present and teaching in the classroom, I don't feel this urgency, but feel dependent upon him to tell me again if I ask him to. Also, I know he will say about the same thing several times anyway." The introspection of this student contains a message of utmost importance and perhaps explains why attention to the screen is greater than attention to the voice of the teacher. Some of the newer approaches to instruction present response situations at frequent intervals and require students to press a button to designate their responses. This necessity to respond at intermittent intervals keeps students alert and motivated. There can be no easy way of hiding from the automatic quality of the machine. Unless a response is made, the light on the individual's panel remains on. Also, some devices record the entire pattern of a student's responses.

Language laboratories have the advantage of requiring each student to make a response. The one-to-one communication possibility between teacher and student provides a stimulating situation, also. The laboratory, with its capacity for several channels of simultaneous operation, allows for a differentiation of content. The potential of the language lab for teaching many content areas has been neglected. Probably that potential, if it were exploited, would have an impact upon many unmotivated students. Not having access to automatic equipment makes it necessary that the teacher create frequent response situations. Research evidence is clear on this point. Frequent interchange between the student and teacher is positively related to classroom learning (Harris 1969).

By their behavior, teachers give direction to students as to the depth of cognitive application a given content is intended to reach. This makes it imperative that forethought be given to the teacher's intent. Is the student only to know and be able to recall a piece of knowledge on demand? If so, this should be communicated in teaching behavior. On the other hand, most academic learning should call for comprehension, application, and deeper levels of cognitive involvement and manipulation. Thus, the teacher needs to engage the students in examining, manipulating, collecting evidence, testing ideas, organizing data, and drawing conclusions. These functions occur only as well as they are planned and guided by the behaviors of the teacher. Assistance in conceptualizing the teaching role in terms of cognitive levels is available in the writing of Jarolimek (1962).

Reinforcement during the learning process has a multidimensional influence to perform. It must do more than provide for the student an external and observable reward or punishment. It has other and more important functions:

(1) **encourages the learner by letting him know he has successfully achieved an intermediate goal;**

(2) **provides pleasure in the learning experience by creating a feeling of rapport between the student and the teacher;**

(3) **clues the learner that he is on either the right or wrong path; and**

(4) **stimulates the search for further reinforcement.**

Handling reinforcement during the conduct of a learning sequence is demanding of the teacher. Different learners require their own kinds of reinforcement. Some children are in need of extrinsic and tangible reinforcers, whereas others need only the clue of "right," "wrong," or "continue." An objective for the teacher ought to be to create the circumstance in which all learners will begin to respond favorably to the intrinsic values of learning and cease to need extrinsic rewards.

Information concerning the effects of certain kinds of reinforcement has been discussed earlier. Specific application to teacher behavior remains to be examined. Examples of several negative reinforcers used by teachers are shown by Symonds (1956). He points out that often these are attacks upon the student's person in the form of statements like:

"Must you be told over and over again?"
"Some children just can't seem to do what they are told."
"No! No! You're not doing it right."
"Can't you ever listen?"

These statements fail in several respects to have their desired effect on the student. As Symonds suggests, they raise emotions, stimulate defensive reactions, and often cause the student to be confused because he does not get from the teacher's remark the information he needs.

Research findings indicate that praise is not as directly related to achievement as had been supposed. *Frequent use of praise* is not as significant in motivation as is *the kind of praise used* (Wallen 1966). The use of mild forms, like saying "uh huh" and "right," are more effective than stronger forms. A finding of a similar nature has been reported by McKeachie (1961) who determined that large amounts of feedback and stimulation interfered with the progress of highly motivated students. French (1958) found that subjects with high motivation respond favorably to objective feedback. For further discussion of this topic, the reader is referred to the work of Spaulding (1965) and Wallen (1966).

Evaluating Learning

A limited view of evaluation as grading has kept teachers confused for much too long. A first step toward emancipation from the tradition that grades are all-important is for educators to become more aware of the varieties and influences of other, and certainly more useful, forms of evaluation. As human beings, we are constantly evaluating as a necessary aspect of relating to our surroundings. And yet, when the term is used in education, there is a tendency to cloak it in formality and shroud it in misconception and anxiety. In fact, evaluation is so closely interwoven with other teaching behaviors, that daily instruction would not take place if all evaluation were removed. This portion of our discussion is intended to show how certain evaluation activities influence motivation.

The way a student, or anyone else, reacts to being evaluated seems to depend upon who is doing the evaluation and upon its potential threat to the person being evaluated. A few general comments about individual reactions to evaluation are important to note. First, the relationship of the evaluator to the person being evaluated partially determines the outcome. Then, it should be noted that anxiety and tension can be the result of placing too much emphasis upon evaluating students. Frequent and matter-of-fact evaluation can become a routine and unemotional thing. However, the least threatening of all is self-evaluation which, in the long run, accomplishes more.

Any model of learning built upon cognition has the concept of evaluation as an integral part. Students and teachers evaluate learning content, processes, and behaviors. Periodically, more formal evaluations of progress take place. At all levels, motivation becomes involved. Unfortunately, it almost always is in the form of concern for grades as extrinsic reinforcers and seldom as intrinsic knowledge of success and failure. When grades are the principal form of evaluation, they stand to lose their influence for many children. Interest has a tendency to wane when there is no hope of acquiring a high grade. There is a tendency for students who get low marks to band together and to give some degree of support to one another. Also, there is a tendency for students to put their energy where the payoff is most immediately rewarding. Consequently, the behaviors teachers use in giving grades have a tendency to lose influence.

Attention must be placed upon self-evaluation if the teacher is to create optimum motivation. How do teachers direct their own behaviors to influence students to evaluate themselves? Again, two ways seem to stand out as being the most effective. First, a teacher, as a model, can allow students to see self-evaluation in action. He can say aloud, "I didn't do that well, did I? I'm sure I can do better if I try again." Students may begin to show similar evaluative behavior if they see that their teachers aren't afraid of it. Secondly, situations calling for self-evaluation can become a part of the classroom experience. During personal conferences, and later, possibly in small groups, the teacher should help the child to evaluate his own learning. This will not occur easily at first, but with practice, improvement will be evident. Amazingly, when students begin to examine their own progress, they seem to gain new momentum. Occasionally, of course, they may become severely disturbed with themselves and may need the encouragement and help of the teacher. But when this is the case, at least the student has a motive to improve, which may not be true when the negative evaluation comes from an external source.

Much has been said by others concerning the motivational influence of grades. Evidence appears to support the conclusion that students expect to get whatever grade they have grown accustomed to receiving. Going back to Sears (1940), findings relating to levels of aspiration and expectancy have been quite consistent. (Ausubel 1955; Uhlinger and Stephens 1960; Todd, Terrell, and Frank 1962). It follows, then, that students who have received low grades are not influenced to aspire to higher grades, and threats of lower grades may not have desirable influences either.

There is now a noticeable trend away from thinking of grades as motivators. Instead, teachers are finding that comments written on papers returned to students have a positive effect. According to Seidman (1967), the nature of the comment makes a difference in this influence. All-inclusive, judgmental comments tend to stifle motivation to improve. Comments which are selective, supportive, and informational tend to increase the probability of improvement.

7

Motivation:
A Continuing Problem

We began on the note that student motivation is a gigantic problem for teachers. Like all serious and far-reaching difficulties, this one requires massive and multidimensional assaults before it can be overcome. Working under the assumption that teachers need all the knowledge and understanding they can acquire, we have reviewed the major concepts and research findings relating to human motivation. We have examined many elements of the educational program in a search for meaningful implications. Finally, teacher behavior, the most significant force in effective education, has been discussed from the viewpoint of student motives. Now it remains for us to ask ourselves how far we have come in the search for an optimum school circumstance—one that maximizes the probability that every student will become an active seeker of learning in the school environment.

Though we are well along in the search for knowledge about human motivation, much remains to be acquired. There are missing parts, and the whole of it must be synthesized into an applicable context. What we know must be translated into applications that are workable in a school program. Achievements in the form of innovative practices must be spread to include students everywhere. In the remaining pages, our discussion turns to a summary of what has been said before as it relates to problems of motivation which remain to be solved.

Motivating the Disadvantaged

There are indications that our society may be entering an era characterized by humanitarian values. Concern for the oppressed and the disadvantaged among us is spreading to the most remote areas of influence. While to the impatient, the change seems to be slow, in reality, the movement is rapid. Fundamental change, of necessity, comes about in terms of people who have themselves accepted human values—not by the dictates of institutions and governments. By their unselfish devotion to human improvement, teachers are among the leaders in responsibility for bringing our society to its present sensibility. Now the school as an institution must have the human resources to multiply the impact of its most resourceful teachers across its entire area of thrust. The resource of greatest importance is knowledge and understanding to guide teachers in their daily pursuit of the goal of improved student functioning.

Improving the lot of an individual without his personal effort and cooperation is next to impossible. We must know how to cause the student most in need of educational help to turn his energy toward achievement. It is obvious that ordinary appeals to motivation are not receiving response. Newly developed programs, while they have produced positive results in some children, have failed to reach the most needy ones. Teachers exhaust their reserves of energy, knowledge, and patience and fail to get the desired results. From where will the answers come? Before we can think in constructive terms, our orientation to the problem must be correct. Our attention must be upon the student as a member of a group of disadvantaged persons and as an individual with unique characteristics. From this orientation, several discrepancies are seen:

1. Our knowledge of the effects of harsh deprivation is by no means complete. What are the emotional and social effects of continued pain and misery associated with poverty? Can the effects, whatever they are, be reversed by application of medical treatments or drugs of some kind? What existing agencies, or new ones, can turn their interest to improving the home situations from which disadvantaged students emerge? Must the sole thrust be the responsibility of the school?

2. What motivational problems are created by early deprivation of sensory stimulation and perceptual training? There are opinions that the curiosity drive is thwarted, or fails to develop, because of it.

3. Does the early lack of success and accomplishment destroy forever the competence motive? If so, we cannot expect the severely disadvantaged child to strive to be adequate and to meet problems with the anticipation of success. If the competence motive is not permanently destroyed, how then, can it be revived and brought to bear on school achievement? Is it possible to develop a controlled environment, a complex machine, into which a child could be placed to develop his competence motive prior to school entrance?

4. Is the affiliation motive damaged or destroyed in children who suffer from severe social rejection by parents and others? If so, what can

be done to revitalize or replace this important source of motivation for school-related activity?

5. What are the educational problems that emerge from language deficiencies, and how can these problems be solved? Can children who have been deprived of adequate language development be taught effectively without having their communication problem become a barrier to learning? Can they grow into improved language patterns? Is it even necessary to have them develop a new language, or should the school develop new learning content using the child's natural communication?

6. Since children from deprived homes seem to function better with tangible rewards, should schools give such rewards? If so, will the social problems thus created be greater than the school can manage? How can children be taken from the point of dependence upon external tangible reinforcers to the point of being satisfied with the intrinsic reinforcement of academic learning?

These are but a few of the many unanswered questions that plague teachers who want to help disadvantaged students. Some tentative answers are beginning to appear in the form of opinions and research. David McClelland (1969) reports success in creating an achievement motive in adults through special training sessions which could be forerunners of new programs for education. Other recent research relating to the psychological characteristics of deprived students have educational implications (Blair 1967; Poussaint and Atkinson 1968; Carpenter and deCharms 1968).

inherent, essential,

Extrinsic to Intrinsic Motivation

To accomplish its other objectives, the school must move children away from dependence upon external reinforcements. One step toward this goal is to isolate those elements of the school that encourage and foster this dependence. Then new techniques and procedures must replace the faulty ones. This process has already begun. Programs of ungrading, team teaching, programmed instruction, and discovery learning embody many of the changes schools must make. Vigorous efforts by educators can spread these programs to touch the lives of students everywhere. New teachers who come into the profession with an awareness of this problem can contribute to its solution, also. They should avoid practices oriented to external reinforcement and should emphasize those techniques which reveal for students the joy and thrill of learning.

Teacher training institutions have a role to play in the accomplishment of this objective. Their curricula and training programs should be examined so as to make sure teacher trainees have the learning opportunities they need. Motivation is a topic which must be given more emphasis in the teacher education program if practitioners are ever to feel secure in facing the motivational problems of their students. At the same time, teachers must learn more about ways of modifying the behaviors they encounter. Knowledge about students and content is not enough. Skill must be acquired. Teachers must manipulate their own behavior in order to bring about the desired behaviors in their students. This calls for training programs built, not around the lectures of professors, but upon self-criticism of goal-directed behavior of the teacher in training.

Interrelationships of Motives

That students have many sources of motivation is a safe assumption to make. That these motives are sometimes supporting and sometimes conflicting is evident to us, also. As yet, however, we know very little about the complex interrelationships among them. When two or more motives come into conflict, we are not able to make reliable predictions of the resultant behavior. Without this information, we are unable to create the group and individual situations most likely to help students resolve their conflicts. We do not know how much to depend upon the affiliation motive as a source of energy for academic learning because we see both supportive and destructive elements within it. We also remain at a loss to know how much competition and how much cooperation to create in the various learning experiences. What are the optimum combinations for individuals and for groups?

Most likely, the answers to questions stimulated by these thoughts must await new and improved measuring devices. A beginning of motivational measurement has been achieved, but many motives remain to be measured. Among the most significant ones, we might include curiosity, manipulation, competence, and self-actualization. Measurements of achievement motivation should be improved and made more usable by the school. The same statement can be made about affiliation motivation. When motives can be said to exist in given strengths on the basis of adequate measurements, then research studies can contribute the knowledge teachers need.

Instructional Media and Motivation

Many statements made about the effectiveness of instructional media are speculative. Research is beginning to tell us something about the motivational influences (McClelland 1969; Saettler 1968), but only in the form of hints that a potential is present. We know that students show boredom when TV instruction is overemphasized. We do not know, however, what the optimum applications of TV and other devices are for arousal and perceptual stimulation. Other questions that remain unanswered are these:

1. What part can instructional devices play in the reinforcement of learning? We know students will work to get visual stimulation, but we have not begun to apply this knowledge to school learning.

2. Can arousal levels be controlled by the intensity of sight and sound to make an optimum situation for learning? Technology holds great potential for studying the relationships among variables of content, arousal, and learning, but we have not begun to explore in this area as yet. Business and advertising have made some assumptions and have built their advertising around various appeals. Possibly educators should become more aware of this approach with the view toward adopting more of it in their own practices.

3. What potential does technology hold for creating whole environments within which students could move about and make responses? Combinations of various media devices have been put into multimedia learning centers, but we know very little about their impact upon motivation and learning. The potential seems to be unlimited and open to intensive investigation.

A Theory of Instruction and Motivation

Educational theorists also have a role to play in the improvement of teaching effectiveness. While several theories are gaining visibility, none seems to have found overwhelming acceptance among teachers. One reason may be that too many aspects of schooling are left out of each theory. Many kinds of behaviors and learnings of students and of teachers must go into a comprehensive view of the school. And any theory must have a core or central theme around which its hypotheses are interwoven. Perhaps, in reality, our discussion in this book has been the advancement of a theory of education built around the theme of student motivation. Certainly we have made some assumptions about motivation that have included many aspects of the total school experience. In the process, perhaps motivation has not been made to stand out as clearly as some readers would like. Therefore, in final summary, these short statements are drawn out of the context of earlier discussion:

1. The motivation that produces behavior is the result of a complex array of interrelated motives.

2. A teacher cannot know the sources and levels of each motive but can observe the behavior resulting from the totality.

3. Natural tendencies of the student to imitate, explore, manipulate, and master his environment are the strongest motives available for school learning.

4. Successful experience intensifies the anticipation and expectancy of future success, and this constitutes a major thrust into and through new learning experiences.

5. Setting goals and standards of excellence for themselves increases students' motivation for achievement.

6. Students have characteristic arousal levels which they seek to maintain.

7. Increases and decreases in arousal level can be induced by controlled circumstances external to the learner.

8. Motivation for school learning is a function of the student interacting with his environment which includes all aspects of the school program as they touch him.

9. Planned movement from extrinsic to intrinsic reinforcement can lead students into a love of learning.

10. Teachers, in their modeling, planning, and conducting behaviors, exercise a significant influence upon student motivation.

It would be strange, indeed, if overnight, teachers began to function with security and confidence in the handling of motivation. A problem as widespread as this one yields only in fractions and only after intense attacks upon it. Schools must change, teachers must learn more and must become more skilled in controlling their own behavior, and the public view of education must be altered in the process of increasing the motivation of students.

Selected References

ALLPORT, G. W. "Attitudes." In *Handbook of Social Psychology*, edited by C. Murchison. Worcester, Mass.: Clark University Press, 1935.
———. "The Functional Autonomy of Motives." *American Journal of Psychology* 50 (1937):141-56.

ALPERT, R., and HABER, R. N. "Anxiety in Academic Achievement Situations." *Journal of Abnormal and Social Psychology* 61 (1960): 207-15.

AMIDON, EDMUND, and HUNTER, ELIZABETH. *Improving Teaching*. New York: Holt, Rinehart & Winston, 1966.

ANGYAL, A. *Foundations for a Science of Personality*. New York: Commonwealth Fund, 1941.

ARGYLE, M., and ROBINSON, P. "Two Origins of Achievement Motivation." *British Journal of Social and Clinical Psychology* 1 (1962): 107-20.

ASSOCIATION FOR SUPERVISION AND CURRICULUM DEVELOPMENT. "Why Group? How Group?" *ASCD News Exchange* 1 (1959):5.

ATKINSON, JOHN W. "Motivational Determinants of Risk-taking Behavior." In *Readings in General Psychology*, edited by W. H. Bartz. Boston: Allyn & Bacon, 1968.

AUSUBEL, D. P. "The Use of Advance Organizers in the Learning and Retention of Meaningful Verbal Material." *Journal of Educational Psychology* 51 (1960):267-72.

———. *The Psychology of Meaningful Verbal Learning*. New York: Grune & Stratton, 1963a.

———. "A Teaching Strategy for Culturally Deprived Pupils: Cognitive and Motivational Considerations." *School Review* 71 (1963b): 454-63.

———. "A Cognitive Structure View of Word and Concept Meaning." In *Readings in the Psychology of Cognition*, edited by R. C. Anderson and D. P. Ausubel. New York: Holt, Rinehart & Winston, 1965.

———. *Educational Psychology: A Cognitive View*. New York: Holt, Rinehart & Winston, 1968.

AUSUBEL, D. P., and SCHIFF, H. M. "A Level of Aspiration Approach to the Measurement of Goal Tenacity." *Journal of General Psychology* 52 (1955):97-110.

AUSUBEL, D. P., and ROBINSON, F. G. *School Learning*. New York: Holt, Rinehart & Winston, 1969.

BANDURA, A., and WALTERS, R. H. "Aggression." *Child Psychology: The Sixty-Second Yearbook of the National Society for the Study of Education*, Part I. Chicago: The National Society for the Study of Education (1963):364-415.

BANDURA, A., and KUPERS, CAROL J. "The Transmission of Patterns of Self-Reinforcement through Modeling." *Journal of Abnormal and Social Psychology* 69 (1964):1-9.

BATTLE, E. S. "Motivational Determinants of Academic Task Persistence." *Journal of Personality and Social Psychology* 4 (1966):634-42.

BEE, HELEN L., and CALLE, HERBERT A. "Effectiveness of Direct Reward and Modeling in Establishment of Standards of Excellence." *Psychological Reports* 23 (1968):1351-58.

BENDER, LAURETTA. "A Visual Motor Gestalt Test and Its Clinical Use." *Research Monograph No. 3*. New York: American Orthopsychiatric Association, 1938.

BERDIE, R. F. "Scores on the Strong Vocational Interest Blank and the Kuder Preference Record in Relation to Self-Ratings." *Journal of Applied Psychology* 34 (1950):42-44.

———. "Aptitude, Achievement, Interest, and Personality Tests: A Longitudinal Comparison." *Journal of Applied Psychology* 39 (1955):103-14.

BERLYNE, D. E. "Stimulus Intensity and Attention in Relation to Learning Theory." *Quarterly Journal of Experimental Psychology* 2 (1950):71-75.

———. "Conflict and Information-Theory Variables as Determinants of Human Perceptual Curiosity." *Journal of Experimental Psychology* 53 (1957): 399-404.

———. *Conflict, Arousal, and Curiosity*. New York: McGraw-Hill Book Co., 1960.

———. "Motivational Problems Raised by Exploratory and Epistemic Behavior." In *Psychology: A Study of a Science*, vol. 5, edited by S. Koch. New York: McGraw-Hill Book Co., 1963.

BEXTON, W. H.; HERON, W.; and SCOTT, T. H. "Effects of Decreased Variation in Sensory Environment." *Canadian Journal of Psychology* 8 (1954):70-76.

BIDDLE, BRUCE J., and ELLENA, WILLIAM, J., ed. *Contemporary Research on Teacher Effectiveness*. New York: Holt, Rinehart & Winston, 1964.

BLAIR, GARLAND E. "The Relationship of Selected Ego Functions and the Academic Achievement of Negro Students." Ph. D. dissertation, Florida State University, 1967.

BLAKE R., and DENNIS, W. "Development of Stereotypes Concerning the Negro." *Journal of Abnormal and Social Psychology* 38 (1943): 525-31.

BOND, GUY L., and DYKSTRA, ROBERT. "The Cooperative Research Program in First Grade Reading Instruction." *Reading Research Quarterly*, IRA, vol. II, no. 4, summer 1967. Newark, Delaware.

BOOCOCK, S. S. "Toward a Sociology of Learning: Peer Group Effects on Student Performance." *Sociology of Education* 39 (1966):26-32.

BORG, WALTER R. *Ability Grouping in the Public Schools*. Madison, Wis.: Dembar Educational Research Services, Inc., 1966.

BROWN, B. FRANK. "The Nongraded High School." *Phi Delta Kappan* 44 (1963):206-9

BRUNER, JEROME S. *The Process of Education*. Cambridge, Mass.: Harvard University Press, 1960.

———. "The Act of Discovery." *Harvard Educational Review* 31 (1961):21-32.

———. "The Course of Cognitive Growth." *American Psychologist* 19 (1964):1-15.

———. "Learning and Thinking." In *Readings in the Psychology of Cognition*, edited by R. C. Anderson and D. C. Ausubel. New York: Holt, Rinehart & Winston, 1965.

BUTLER, R. A. "The Effect of Deprivation of Visual Incentives on Visual Exploration Motivation in Monkeys." *Journal of Comparative Physiological Psychology* 50:177-79.

CANNON, W. B. *The Wisdom of the Body*. New York: W. W. Norton & Co., 1932.

CARPENTER, V., and deCHARMS, R. "Measuring Motivation in Culturally Disadvantaged School Children." *Journal of Experimental Education* 37 (1968):31-41.

CARTWRIGHT, D. "The Effect of Interruption, Completion, and Failure upon the Attractiveness of Activities." *Journal of Experimental Psychology* 31 (1942):1-16.

CAWELTI, GORDON. "High School Ability Grouping Programs." *Bulletin of the National Association of Secondary School Principals* 47 (1963):34-39.

CHATTERTON, ROLAND. "Interdisciplinary Learning of Social Studies." *Audiovisual Instruction* 14 (1969):27-28.

CHILD, I. L., and WHITING, J. W. "Determination of Level of Aspiration: Evidence from Everyday Life." *Journal of Abnormal and Social Psychology* 44 (1949):303-14.

CLARK, BARBARA S. "The Acquisition and Extinction of Peer Imitation in Children." *Psychonomic Science* 2 (1965):147-48.

CLARKE, E. C. "Factors Relating to Underachievement." *School and Community* 49 (1962):22-23.

CLARKE, WENTWORTH. "Simulation for Stimulation." *Audiovisual Instruction* 14 (1969):44-48.

COLEMAN, JAMES S. *The Adolescent Society*. New York: Free Press, 1961.

COLLEGE ENTRANCE EXAMINATION BOARD. *A Guide to the Advanced Placement Program, 1964-65*. Princeton, N. J.

COMBS, A. W. "A Method for Analysis for the Thematic Apperception Test and Autobiography." *Journal of Clinical Psychology* 2 (1946): 167-74.

―――. "The Personal Approach to Good Teaching." *Educational Leadership* 21 (1964):369-77.

―――. "Fostering Self-Direction." *Educational Leadership* 23 (1966): 373-76.

CONNELLY, JEANNE. "Making Pupils Aware of Why They Write." *Chicago Schools Journal* 37 (1956):222-24.

CRAIG, R. C. "Recent Research on Discovery." *Educational Leadership* 26 (1969):501-5.

CRANDALL, V. C.; GOOD, S.; and CRANDALL, V. J. "Reinforcement Effects of Adult Reactions and Nonreactions on Children's Achievement Expectations: A Replication Study." *Child Development* 35 (1964):485-97.

CRANDALL, V. C., and MCGHEE, PAUL E. "Expectancy of Reinforcement and Academic Competence." *Journal of Personality* 36 (1968): 635-48.

CROWDER, NORMAN A. "On the Differences between Linear and Intrinsic Programming." *Phi Delta Kappan* 44 (1963):250-54.

DAVISON, DEWITT C. "Some Demographic and Attitudinal Concomitants of the Perceived Reward Value of Classroom Reinforcement: An Application of Newcomb's Balance Theory." Ph. D. dissertation. University of Illinois, 1967.

DEMBER W. N.; NAIRNE, F.; and MILLER, F. J. "Further Validation of the Alpert-Haber Achievement Anxiety Test." *Journal of Abnormal and Social Psychology* 65 (1962):427-28.

DOOB, L. W. "The Behavior of Attitudes." In *Human Learning*, edited by A. W. Staats, pp. 295-306. New York: Holt, Rinehart & Winston, 1964.

DOUVAN, ELIZABETH. "Social Status and Success Strivings." *Journal of Abnormal and Social Psychology* 52 (1956):219-23.

DREIKURS, RUDOLF. *Psychology in the Classroom*. 2d ed. New York: Harper & Row, 1968.

DRISCOLL, PATRICK A. "A Summer Remedial Program for Primary Children." *The National Elementary Principal* 48 (1969):43-44.

DUFFY, ELIZABETH. "The Nature and Development of the Concept of Activation." In *Current Research in Motivation*, edited by Ralph N. Haber. New York: Holt, Rinehart & Winston, 1966.

EDUCATIONAL POLICIES COMMISSION. *The Central Purpose of American Education*. Washington, D. C.: National Education Association, 1961.

EISNER, ELLIOT W. "Qualitative Intelligence and the Act of Teaching." *Elementary School Journal* 63 (1963):299-307.

ELLIOTT, P., and MOUSTAKAS, C. E. "Free Emotional Expression in the Classroom." *Progressive Education* 28 (1951):125-28.

FEATHER, N. T. "Subjective Probability and Decision under Uncertainty." *Psychological Review* 66 (1959):150-64.

―――. "The Effect of Differential Failure on Expectation of Success, Reported Anxiety, and Response Uncertainty." *Journal of Personality* 31 (1963):289-312.

―――. "Effects of Prior Success and Failure on Expectations of Success and Subsequent Performance." *Journal of Personality and Social Psychology* 3 (1966):287-98.

FESTINGER, L. "Wish, Expectation, and Group Standards as Factors Influencing Level of Aspiration." *Journal of Abnormal and Social Psychology* 37 (1942):184-200.

―――. "Motivations Leading to Social Behavior." In *The Nebraska Symposium on Motivation*, edited by R. Marshall. Lincoln: University of Nebraska Press, 1954.

―――. *A Theory of Cognitive Dissonance*. Stanford, Calif.: Stanford University Press, 1957.

―――. "The Psychological Effects of Insufficient Rewards." In *Readings in General Psychology*, edited by W. H. Bartz. Boston: Allyn & Bacon, 1968.

FISKE, D. W., and MADDI, S. R. "A Conceptual Framework." In *Functions of Varied Experience*, edited by D. W. Fiske and S. R. Maddi, pp. 11-56. Homewood, Ill.: Dorsey Press, 1961.

FLANDERS, N. A. *Teacher Influence, Pupil Attitudes, and Achievement*. U. S. Department of Health, Education and Welfare, Office of Education, Cooperative Research Monography No. 12. Washington, D. C.: Government Printing Office, 1965.

FLUGEL, J. C. *The Psychoanalytic Study of the Family*. London: Hogarth Press, 1926.

FOWLER, H. "Response to Environmental Change: A Positive Replication." *Psychological Reports* 4 (1958):506.

————. *Curiosity and Exploratory Behavior*. New York: Macmillan Co., 1965.

FRANKEL, CHARLES. "Appearance and Reality in Kilpatrick's Philosophy." *Teachers College Record* 66 (1965):352-64.

FRANSETH, JANE. "A Review of Research in Grouping." *School Life* 45 (1963):5-6.

FRENCH, ELIZABETH G. "The Interaction of Achievement Motivation and Ability in Problem-Solving Success." *Journal of Abnormal and Social Psychology* 57 (1958):306-9.

FULL, HAROLD. *Controversy in American Education*. New York: Macmillan Co., 1967.

FUSTER, JOAQUIN M. "Effects of Stimulation of Brain Stem on Tachistoscopic Perception." *Science* 127 (1958):150.

GAGE, N. L. *Handbook of Research on Teaching*. Chicago: Rand McNally & Co., 1963.

GANS, ROMA. *Common Sense in Teaching Reading*. Indianapolis: Bobbs-Merrill Co., 1963.

GARDNER, J. W. "The Use of the Term 'Level of Aspiration.' " *Psychological Review* 47 (1940):59-68.

GARRY, RALPH J. *Report of Research on the Integration of Science Teaching by Television into the Elementary Program*. Boston University, 1960.

GOODLAD, JOHN I. "The Organizing Center in Curriculum Theory and Practice." *Theory into Practice* 1 (1962):215-21.

————. "Nongraded Schools: Meeting Children Where They Are." *Saturday Review* 48 (1965):57-59, 72-74.

————. "Diagnosis and Prescription in Educational Practice." *New Approaches to Individualizing Instruction*. Princeton, N. J., Educational Testing Service, 1966.

————. "The Educational Program to 1980 and Beyond." In *Designing Education for the Future II*, edited by E. L. Morphett and C. O. Ryan, pp. 47-60. New York: Citation Press, 1967.

GOWAN, J. C. "Intelligence, Interests, and Reading Ability in Relation to Scholastic Achievement." *Psychological Newsletter* 8 (1957): 85-87.

GRAFFAM, DONALD T. "Why Not Team Learning?" *Journal of Teacher Education* 15 (1964):289-92.

GRANIT, R. "Brain Control of the Sense Organs." *Acta Psychology* 11 (1955):117-18.

GRANZOW, K. R. "A Comparative Study of Underachievers, Normal Achievers, and Overachievers in Reading." Ph. D. dissertation, State University of Iowa, 1954.

GREEN, ROBERT L., and STACKNICK, T. J. "Money, Motivation, and Academic Achievement." *Phi Delta Kappan* 50 (1968):228-30.

GREENBAUM, C. W.; COHN, A.; and KRAUSS, R. M. "Choice, Negative Information and Attractiveness of Tasks." *Journal of Personality* 33 (1965):46-59.

GRIMES, J. W., and ALLINSMITH, W. "Compulsivity, Anxiety and School Achievement." *Merrill-Palmer Quarterly* 7 (1961):247-69.

GRUSEC, JOAN, and MISCHEL, W. "Models' Characteristics as Determinants of Social Learning." *Journal of Personality and Social Psychology* 4 (1966):211-15.

HALL, J. F. *Psychology of Motivation*. Philadelphia: J. B. Lippincott Co., 1961.

HARRIS, ALBERT J. "The Effective Teacher of Reading." Paper presented to International Reading Association, Kansas City, Mo., May 1, 1969.

HEBB, D. O. "Drives and the C. N. S. (Conceptual Nervous System)." *The Psychological Review* 62 (1955):243-54.

HECKHAUSEN, HEINZ. *The Anatomy of Achievement Motivation*. New York: Academic Press, 1967.

HEILBRUN, ALFRED B., and WATERS, DAVID B. "Underachievement as Related to Perceptual Maternal Child Rearing and Academic Conditions of Reinforcement." *Child Development* 39 (1968):913-21.

HENDRIX, GERTRUDE. "Learning by Discovery." *The Mathematics Teacher* 54 (1961):290-99.

HERRICK, VIRGIL E. "Curriculum Decisions and Provision for Individual Differences." *Elementary School Journal* 62 (1968):313-21.

HILGARD, ERNEST R. "A Perspective on the Relationship between Learning Theory and Educational Practices." *Theories of Learning and Instruction*. Yearbook of the National Society for the Study of Education 63 (1964):part I, 402-18.

HILL, W. F. "Activity as an Autonomous Drive." *Journal of Comparative and Physiological Psychology* 49 (1956):15-19.

HIPPLE, THEODORE W. "Participatory Education—Students Assist Teachers." *National Association of Secondary School Principals Bulletin* 53 (1969):80-89.

HOFFMAN, M. L.; MITSOS, S. B.; and PROTZ, R. E. "Achievement Striving, Social Class, and Test Anxiety." *Journal of Abnormal and Social Psychology* 56 (1958):401-3.

HOROWITZ, E. L., and HOROWITZ, R. E. "Development of Social Attitudes in Children." *Sociometry* 1 (1938):301-38.

HUGHES, MARIE M. "Utah Study of the Assessment of Teaching." In *Theory and Research in Teaching*, edited by A. A. Bellack. New York: Bureau of Publication, Teachers College, Columbia University, 1963.

HULL, C. L. *Principles of Behavior*. New York: Appleton-Century-Crofts, 1943.

HUNT, J. McV. *Intelligence and Experience*. New York: Ronald Press Co., 1951.

————. "Experience and the Development of Motivation: Some Reinterpretations." *Child Development* 31 (1960):489-504.

————. "Motivation Inherent in Information Processing and Action." In *Motivation and Social Organization: The Cognitive Factors*, edited by O. J. Harvey. New York: Ronald Press Co., 1963.

————. "The Epigenesis of Intrinsic Motivation and Early Cognitive Learning." In *Current Research in Motivation*, edited by R. N. Haber. New York: Holt, Rinehart & Winston, 1966.

INGRAHAM, LEONARD W. "New Strategies and Roles for the Social Studies Teacher." *Audiovisual Instruction* 14 (1969):24-25.

INSKEEP, JAMES, and ROWLAND, MONROE. "An Analysis of School Subject Preferences of Elementary School Children of the Middle Grades: Another Look." *Journal of Educational Research* 58 (1965):225-28.

ITA, SISTER MARY. "Diagnosing Causes of Prejudices of Children in School." *National Catholic Education Association Bulletin* (1950): 441-44.

ITKIN, W. "Relationships between Attitudes toward Parents and Parent Attitudes toward Children." *Journal of Genetic Psychology* 86 (1955):339-53.

JACOBS, J. N.; GRATE, J. H.; and DOWNING, U. M. "Do Methods Make a Difference in Educational Television?" *The Elementary School Journal* 63 (1963):248-54.

JAKUBCZAK, L. F., and WALTERS, R. H. "Suggestibility as Dependency Behavior." *Journal of Abnormal and Social Psychology* 59 (1959): 102-7.

JAMES, WILLIAM. *The Principles of Psychology*, vol. I. New York: Henry Holt & Co., 1890.

JAROLIMEK, JOHN. "The Taxonomy: Guide to Differentiated Instruction." *Social Education* 26 (1962):445-47.

JERSILD, ARTHUR T. "Emotional Development." In *Educational Psychology*, 4th ed. edited by C. E. Skinner. Englewood Cliffs, N. J.: Prentice-Hall, 1959.

JERSILD, ARTHUR T., and TASCH, R. J. *Children's Interests and What They Suggest for Education*. New York: Bureau of Publications, Teachers College, Columbia University, 1949.

JONES, R. STEWART. "Ability Grouping and Related Issues." *Review of Educational Research* 36 (1966):419-20.

JOUVET, M. "Etude Neuro Physiologique Chez l'Homme de Quelques Mechanismes Sous-Corticaux de l'Attention." *Psychology Française* 2 (1957):254-60.

JUCKNAT, M. "Leistung, Anspruchsniveau und Selbstbewusstsein." *Psychologische Forschung* 22 (1937):89-179.

KAGAN, J., and MOSS, H. A. *Birth to Maturity*. New York: John Wiley & Sons, 1962.

KAUFMAN, M. M. *Expressed Interests of Children in Relation to a Maturity Age Index in Grades Four through Eight*. Ph. D. dissertation, Northwestern University, 1955.

KELIHER, ALICE V. "Effective Learning and Teacher-Pupil Ratio." *Childhood Education* 43 (1966):3-6.

KIESTER, M. E. "The Behavior of Young Children in Failure: An Experimental Attempt to Discover and Modify Responses of Preschool Children to Failure." *University of Iowa Studies in Child Welfare* 14 (1938):27-82.

KIGHT, HOWARD R., and SASSENRATH, JULIUS M. "Relation of Achievement Motivation and Text Anxiety to Performance in Programmed Instruction." *Journal of Educational Psychology* 57 (1966):14-17.

KIVY, P. N.; EARL, R. W.; and WALKER, E. L. "Stimulus Context and Satiation." *Journal of Comparative Physiological Psychology* 49 (1956):90-92.

KOCH, H. L. "The Relation of Certain Family Constellation Characteristics and the Attitudes of Children toward Adults." *Child Development* 26 (1955):13-40.

KOFFKA, K. *Principles of Gestalt Psychology*. New York: Harcourt, Brace & World, 1935.

KRICH, PERCY. "Room 23 Weekly—A Creative Writing Experience." *Elementary School Journal* 63 (1963):336-41.

KROUT, M. H., and STAGNER, R. "Personality Development in Radicals: A Comparative Study." *Sociometry* 2 (1939):31-46.

KURTZ, J. J., and SWENSON, ESTER, J. "Factors Related to Overachievement and Underachievement in School." *School Review* 59 (1951):472-80.

LACEY, J. C. "Does Teaching Change Students' Attitudes?" *Journal of Educational Research* 50 (1956):307-11.

LASSWELL, H. D. *Psychopathology and Politics*. Chicago: University of Chicago Press, 1930.

LEIDY, T. R., and STARRY, A. B. "The American Adolescent—A Bewildering Amalgam." *NEA Journal* 56 (1967):8-12.

LIEBERT, R. M., and ALLEN, M. K. "Effects of Role Structure and Reward Magnitude on the Acquisition and Adoption of Self-Reward Criteria." *Psychological Reports* 21 (1967):445-52.

LIEBERT, R. M., and ORA, JOHN P. "Children's Adoption of Self-Reward Patterns: Incentive Level and Method of Transmission." *Child Development* 39 (1968):537-44.

LINDSLEY, O. R. "Operant Conditioning Methods Applied to Research on Chronic Schizophrenics." *Psychiatric Research Reports* 5 (1956):118-39.

LIPPIT, R., and CLANCY, C. "Psychodrama in the Kindergarten and Nursery School." *Group Psychotherapy* 7 (1954):262-90.

MCCLELLAND, D. C. "The Role of Educational Technology in Developing Achievement Motivation." *Educational Technology* (1969): 7-16.

MCCLELLAND, D. C.; CLARK, R. A; ROBY, T. B.; and ATKINSON, J. W. "The Effect of the Need for Achievement on Thematic Apperception." *Journal of Experimental Psychology* 37 (1949): 242-55.

MCCLELLAND, D. C.; DAVID, C.; ATKINSON, J. W.; CLARK, RUSSELL A.; and LOWELL, EDGAR L. *The Achievement Motive*. New York: Appleton-Century-Crofts, 1953.

MCKEACHIE, W. J. "Motivation, Teaching Methods, and College Learning." In *Nebraska Symposium on Motivation*, edited by M. R. Jones, pp. 111-42. Lincoln: University of Nebraska Press, 1961.

MCNALLY, H. J., and PASSOW, A. H. *Improving the Quality of Public School Programs*. New York: Bureau of Publications, Teachers College, Columbia University, 1960.

MCNAMARA, H. J.; SOLLEY, C. M.; and LONG, J. "The Effects of Punishment (Electric Shock) on Perceptual Learning." *Journal of Abnormal and Social Psychology* 57 (1958):91-98.

MADDI, S. R. "Motivational Aspects of Creativity." *Journal of Personality* 33 (1965):330-47.

MALMO, ROBERT B. "Activation: A Neuropsychological Dimension." *Psychological Review* 66 (1959):367-86.

MANDLER, G., and SARASON, S. R. "A Study of Anxiety and Learning." *Journal of Abnormal and Social Psychology* 47 (1952):166-73.

MANGAN, G. L. "The Role of Punishment in Figure-Ground Reorganization." *Journal of Experimental Psychology* 58 (1959):369-75.

MARSHALL, H. H. "The Effect of Punishment on Children: A Review of the Literature and a Suggested Hypothesis." *Journal of Genetic Psychology* 106 (1965):23-33.

———. "Learning as a Function of Task Interest Reinforcement and Social Class Variables." Ph. D. dissertation, University of California, Berkeley, 1967.

MARTIRE J. G. "Relationships between the Self-Concept and Differences in the Strength and Generality of Achievement Motivation." *Journal of Personality* 24 (1956):364-75.

MARUZZI, G., and MAGOUN, H. W. "Brain Stem Reticular Formation and Activation of the EEG." *EEG Clinical Neurophysiology* 1 (1949): 455-73.

MARX, MELVIN H., and TOMBAUGH, TOM N. *Motivation*. San Francisco: Chandler Publishing Co., 1967.

MASLOW, A. H. "A Theory of Motivation." *Psychological Review* 50 (1943):370-96.

―――. *Motivation and Personality*. New York: Harper & Row, Publishers, 1954.

―――. "Deficiency Motivation and Growth Motivation." In *The Nebraska Symposium on Motivation*, edited by M. R. Jones. Lincoln: University of Nebraska Press, 1955.

MAW, W. H., and MAW, E. W. "Selections of Unbalanced and Unusual Designs by Children High in Curiosity." *Child Development* 33 (1962):917:22.

MEDLEY, D. M., and MITZELL, H. E. "A Technique for Measuring Classroom Behavior." *Journal of Educational Psychology* 49 (1958):86-92.

MENDEL, GISELA. "Children's Preferences for Differing Degrees of Novelty." *Child Development* 36 (1965):453-65.

METCALF, L. E. "Attitudes and Beliefs as Materials of Instruction." *Progressive Education* 27 (1950):127-29.

MILLER, N. E. "Studies of Fear as an Acquired Drive: I. Fear as Motivation and Fear Reduction as Reinforcement in the Learning of New Responses." *Journal of Experimental Psychology* 38 (1948):89-101.

MILLER, N. E., and DOLLARD, J. *Social Learning and Imitation*. New Haven, Conn.: Yale University Press, 1941.

MOSS, F. A. "A Study of Animal Drives." *Journal of Experimental Psychology* 7 (1924):165-85.

MOWRER, O. H. *Learning Theory and Behavior*. New York: John Wiley & Sons, 1960.

MULLER, PHILIPPE. *The Tasks of Childhood*. New York: McGraw-Hill Book Co., 1969.

MUNZ, DAVID C.; SMOUSE, ALBERT D.; and LETCHWORTH, GEORGE. "Achievement Motivation and Ordinal Position of Birth." *Psychological Reports* 23 (1968):175-80.

MURRAY, H. A. *Explorations in Personality*. New York: Oxford University Press, 1938.

―――. *Thematic Apperception Test Manual*. Cambridge, Mass.: Harvard University Press, 1943.

MUSSEN, P. H. "Some Personality and Social Factors Related to Changes in Children's Attitudes toward Negroes." *Journal of Abnormal and Social Psychology* 45 (1950):432-41.

MUSSEN, P. H., and JONES, MARY C. "The Behavior—Inferred Motivations of Late and Early Maturing Boys." *Child Development* 29 (1958): 61-67.

MUSSEN, P. H., and PORTER, L. W. "Personal Motivation and Self-Conceptions Associated with Effectiveness and Ineffectiveness in Emergent Groups." *Journal of Abnormal and Social Psychology* 59 (1959):23-27.

NASH, R. "A Study of Particular Self-Perceptions as Related to Scholastic Achievement of Junior High Age Pupils in a Middle-Class Community." Ph. D. dissertation, Rutgers University, 1963.

NATIONAL EDUCATION ASSOCATION. *The Scholars Look at the Schools*. Washington, D. C.: National Education Association, 1962.

NEWCOMB, T. M. *Personality and Social Change*. New York: Dryden Press, 1943.

NICHOLS, H. "Role-Playing in Primary Grades." *Group Psychotherapy* 7 (1954):238-41.

NICHOLSON, W. M. "The Influence of Anxiety upon Learning." *Journal of Personality* 26 (1958):303-19.

NISSEN, H. W. "A Study of Exploratory Behavior in the White Rat by Means of the Obstruction Method." *Journal of Genetic Psychology* 37 (1930):361-76.

PAGE, ELLIS B. "Teacher Comments and Student Performance." *Journal of Educational Psychology* 49 (1958):173-81.

PETERS, R. S. *The Concept of Motivation*. New York: Humanities Press, 1960.

POIRIER, GERARD A. "An Evaluation of Team Learning in a Fourth Grade." Ph. D. dissertation, University of California, Berkeley, 1967.

POUSSAINT, ALVIN F., and ATKINSON, CAROLYN O. "Negro Youth and Psychological Motivation." *Journal of Negro Education* 37 (1968):241-51.

REMAVICH, ROSE, and ZILINSKY, PIETER. "Enrichment for Everyone." *Elementary School Journal* 63 (1963):317-23.

RIBBLE, MARGARET. "Infantile Experience in Relation to Personality and Behavior." In *Personality and the Behavior Disorders*, vol. II, edited by J. McV. Hunt. New York: Ronald Press Co., 1944.

RICHTER, ANITA. "Gifted Children Grow through Library Project." *Chicago Schools Journal* 44 (1962):78-82.

RIPPEY, ROBERT M. "Fitting Research on Instruction into the Conceptual Model." Paper read to APA, 1965.

ROBINSON, J. "Light as a Reinforcer for Bar Pressing in Rats as a Function of Adaptation, Illumination Level and Direction of Light Change." *American Psychologist* (Abstract) 12 (1957):411.

———. "Light Onset and Termination as Reinforcers for Rats under Normal Light Conditions." *Psychological Reports* 5 (1959):793:96.

———. "The Reinforcing Effects of Response—Contingent Light Increment and Decrement in Hooded Rats." *Journal of Comparative Physiological Psychology* 54 (1961):470-73.

RODGERS, FREDERICK A. "To Think, to Learn, to Act." *Educational Leadership* 25 (1968):158-60.

ROE, ANNE. "Early Determinants of Vocational Choice." *Journal of Counseling Psychology* 4 (1957):212-17.

ROGERS, CARL R. "The Facilitation of Significant Learning." In *Instruction: Some Contemporary Viewpoints*, edited by Laurence Siegel, pp. 37-54. San Francisco: Chandler Publishing Co., 1967.

ROSEN, BERNARD C., and D'ANDRADE, ROY. "The Psychosocial Origins of Achievement Motivation." *Sociometry* 22 (1959):185-218.

ROSENZWEIG, S. "Preferences in the Repetition of Successful and Unsuccessful Activities as a Function of Age and Personality." *Journal of Genetic Psychology* 42 (1933):423-41.

ROUDINESCO, J. "Severe Maternal Deprivation and Personality Development in Early Childhood." *Understanding the Child* 21 (1952):104.

RUSSELL, I. L. "Attitudes, Interests, and Values." In *Educational Psychology*. 4th ed. Edited by C. E. Skinner. Englewood Cliffs, N. J.: Prentice-Hall, 1959.

————. "Motivation for School Achievement: Measurement and Validation." *Journal of Educational Research* 62 (1969):263-66.

SAETTLER, PAUL. *A History of Instructional Technology*. New York: McGraw-Hill Book Co., 1968.

SARASON, S. B., et al. *Anxiety in Elementary School Children*. New York: John Wiley & Sons, 1960.

SCHAFER, R., and MURPHY, G. "The Role of Autism in a Visual Figure-Ground Relationship." *Journal of Experimental Psychology* 32 (1943):335-43.

SCHUCK, R. F. "The Effects of Set Induction upon Pupil Achievement, Retention, and Assessment of Effective Teaching in a Unit on Respiration in the BSCS Curricula." *Educational Leadership* 26 (1969):785-93.

SCHWAB, J. J. "The Teaching of Science as Inquiry." *The Teaching of Science*. Cambridge, Mass.: Harvard University Press, 1962.

SEARS, PAULINE S. "Levels of Aspiration in Academically Successful and Unsuccessful Children." *Journal of Abnormal and Social Psychology* 35 (1940):498-536.

SEARS, PAULINE S., and HILGARD, E. R. "The Teacher's Role in the Motivation of the Learner." *Theories of Learning and Instruction*. Yearbook of NSSE, 63, Part I (1964):182-209.

SEIDMAN, EARL. "Marking Students' Compositions: Implications of Achievement Motivation Theory." Ph. D. dissertation, Stanford University, 1967.

SHAFTEL, F. R.; CRABTREE, C.; and RUSHWORTH, V. "Problem-solving in the Elementary School." In *Problems Approach in the Social Studies*, edited by R. E. Gross, pp. 25-47. Washington, D. C.: National Education Association, 1960.

SHAPLIN, J. T., and OLDS, H. F., ed. *Team Teaching.* New York: Harper & Row, Publishers, 1964.

SIEGEL, L., and SIEGEL, L. C. "Educational Set: A Determiner of Acquisition." *Journal of Educational Psychology* 56 (1965):1-12.

SKINNER, B. F. *The Technology of Teaching.* New York: Appleton-Century-Crofts, 1968.

SMOCK, C. D., and HOLT, B. G. "Children's Reactions to Novelty: An Experimental Study of Curiosity Motivation." *Child Development* 33 (1962):631-42.

SNYGG, DONALD, and COMBS, ARTHUR W. *Individual Behavior.* New York: Harper & Row, Publishers, 1949.

SPAULDING, R. L. *Achievement, Creativity, and Self-Concept Correlates of Teacher-Pupil Interaction in Elementary Schools.* Cooperative Research Project No. 1352. Hempstead, N. Y.: Hoffstra University, 1965.

SPENCE, K. W., and FARBER, I. E. "Conditioning and Extinction as a Function of Anxiety." *Journal of Experimental Psychology* 45 (1953):116-19.

SPENCE, K. W., and TAYLOR, JANET A. "The Relation of Conditioned Response Strength to Anxiety in Normal, Neurotic, and Psychotic Subjects." *Journal of Experimental Psychology* 45 (1953):265-72.

SPITZ, R. A. "The Psychogenic Diseases in Infancy: An Attempt at Their Etiological Classification." *Psychoanalytic Study of the Child* 6 (1951):255-75.

STAGNER, ROSS. "Studies of Aggressive Social Attitudes. III. Role of Personal and Family Scores." *Journal of Social Psychology* 20 (1944): 129-40.

———. *Psychology of Personality.* New York: McGraw-Hill Book Co., 1948.

STEINER, IVAN D. "Self-Perception and Goal-Setting Behavior." *Journal of Personality* 25 (1957):344-55.

STEISEL, I. M., and COHEN, B. D. "The Effect of Two Degrees of Level of Failure on Level of Aspiration and Performance." *Journal of Abnormal and Social Psychology* 46 (1951):79-82.

STOLUROW, L. M. "Let's Be Informed on Programmed Instruction." *Phi Delta Kappan* 44 (1963):255-57.

SUCHMAN, J. R. "Inquiry Training: Building Skills for Autonomous Discovery." *Merrill-Palmer Quarterly of Behavior and Development* 7 (1961):148-69.

SUPER, D. E. *Appraising Vocational Fitness.* New York: Harper & Row, Publishers, 1949.

———. *The Psychology of Careers.* New York: Harper & Row, Publishers, 1957.

SYMONDS, PERCIVAL M. "What Education Has to Learn from Psychology." *Teachers College Record* 57 (1956):449-62.

TAYLOR, JANET A. "A Personality Scale of Manifest Anxiety." *Journal of Abnormal and Social Psychology* 48 (1953):285-90.

———. "Drive Theory and Manifest Anxiety." *Psychological Bulletin* 53 (1956):303-20.

TAYLOR, JANET A., and SPENCE, K. W. "The Relationship of Anxiety Level to Performance in Serial Learning." *Journal of Experimental Psychology* 44 (1952):61-64.

TERRELL, G. "Manipulatory Motivation in Children." *Journal of Comparative Physiological Psychology* 52 (1959):705-9.

TERRELL, G.; DURKIN, J.; and WIESLEY, M. "Social Class and the Nature of the Incentive in Discrimination Learning." *Journal of Abnormal and Social Psychology* 59 (1959):270-72.

THORNDIKE, E. L. *Educational Psychology, vol. II., The Psychology of Learning*. New York: Teachers College, Columbia University, 1913.

———. *The Fundamentals of Learning*. New York: Teachers College, Columbia University, 1932.

TODD, F. J.; TERRELL, G; and FRANK, C. E. "Differences between Normal and Underachievers of Superior Ability." *Journal of Applied Psychology* 46 (1962):183-90.

TOLMAN, E. C. *Purposive Behavior in Animals and Men*. New York: Appleton-Century-Crofts, 1932.

TRAVERS, ROBERT M. W. *Essentials of Learning*. New York: Macmillan Co., 1967.

TRUMP, J. LLOYD. "What Is Team Teaching?" *Education* 85 (1965): 327-32.

TYLER, L. E. "The Relationship of Interests to Abilities and Reputation among Fifth Grade Children." *Educational and Psychological Measurement* 11 (1951):255-64.

———. "The Development of Vocational Interest: The Organization of Likes and Dislikes in Ten-Year-Old Children." *Journal of Genetic Psychology* 86 (1955):33-44.

UHLINGER, C. A., and STEPHENS, M. W. "Relation of Achievement Motivation to Academic Achievement in Students of Superior Ability." *Journal of Educational Psychology* 51 (1960):259-66.

WALKER, E. L. "Psychological Complexity as a Basis for a Theory of Motivation and Choice." In *Nebraska Symposium on Motivation*, edited by David Levine. Lincoln: University of Nebraska Press, 1964.

WALLACE, WALTER L. "Peer Influences and Undergraduates' Aspirations for Graduate Study." *Sociology of Education* 38 (1965): 377-92.

WALLEN, N. E. *Relationship between Teacher Characteristics and Student Behavior, Part 3.* Cooperative Research Project No. SAE OE5-10-181. Salt Lake City: University of Utah, 1966.

WEINBERG, CARL. "The Price of Competition." *Teachers College Record* 67 (1965):106-14.

WEINER, BERNARD. "Effects of Unsatisfied Achievement Motivation on Persistence and Subject Performance." *Journal of Personality* 33 (1965):428-42.

WEIR, E. C. "The Meaning of Learning and the Learning of Meaning." *Phi Delta Kappan* 46 (1965):280-84.

WENDT, H. W. "Risk-taking as a Function of Preverbal Imprinting? Some Data and Speculations." *Archives of Gestalt Psychology* 113 (1961):325-50.

WHITE, R. W. "Motivation Reconsidered: The Concept of Competence." *Psychological Review* 66 (1959):297-333.

——. "Motivation Reconsidered: The Concept of Competence." In *Studies in Educational Psychology*, edited by Raymond G. Kuhlen. Waltham, Mass.: Ginn/Blaisdell, 1968.

WHITING, J. W. M., and MOWRER, O. H. "Habit Progression and Regression—A Laboratory Study of Some Factors Relevant to Human Socialization." *Journal of Comparative Psychology* 36 (1943): 229-53.

WILLIAMS, ASTON R. *General Education in Higher Education.* New York: Teachers College Press, Columbia University, 1968.

WILLIAMS, C. D., and KUCHTA, J. C. "Exploratory Behavior in Two Mazes with Dissimilar Alternatives." *Journal of Comparative Physiological Psychology* 50 (1957):509-13.

WINTERBOTTOM, MARIAN R. "The Relation of Need for Achievement to Learning Experiences in Independence and Mastery." In *Motives in Fantasy Action and Society*, edited by J. W. Atkinson, pp. 453-78. New York: Van Nostrand Reinhold Co., 1958.

WITHALL, JOHN. "The Development of a Technique for the Measurement of Social-Emotional Climate in Classrooms." *Journal of Experimental Education* 17 (1949):347-61.

YOUNG, P. T. "Studies of Food Preference, Appetite, and Dietary Habits. I. Running Activity and Dietary Habit of the Rat in Relation to Food Preference." *Journal of Comparative Psychology* 37 (1944): 327-70.

ZIGLER, EDWARD, and DELABRY, JACQUES. "Concept-Switching Behavior in Middle-Class, Lower-Class, and Retarded Children." *Journal of Abnormal and Social Psychology* 65 (1962):267-72.

Index